**HOCKEY** HOW TO PLAY LIKE THE PROS

# HOCKEY
## HOW TO PLAY LIKE THE PROS

**SEAN ROSSITER**
**& PAUL CARSON**

GREYSTONE BOOKS

Douglas & McIntyre Publishing Group

Vancouver/Toronto/Berkeley

To my father, John Carson, who planted the "seed of hockey" in my life very early on, and served as an inspirational role model along the way.
**PAUL CARSON**

To Capt. Alex Rossiter, who at age 36 captained one of the Canadian Army teams based in Germany that played the World Hockey Champion Penticton Vees in March 1955. They lost 11–3, but scored three more goals than the air force did.
**SEAN ROSSITER**

Copyright © 2004 by Sean Rossiter and Paul Carson

04 05 06 07 08   5 4 3 2 1

Greystone Books
A division of Douglas & McIntyre Ltd.
2323 Quebec Street, Suite 201
Vancouver, British Columbia
Canada  V5T 4S7
www.greystonebooks.com

*National Library of Canada Cataloguing in Publication Data*
Rossiter, Sean, 1946–
 Hockey : how to play like the pros / Sean Rossiter & Paul Carson.
 (Hockey the NHL way)
 ISBN 1-55365-044-1

 1. Hockey—Juvenile literature. I. Carson, Paul, 1955– II. Title. III. Series.
GV847.25.R678 2004 j796.962'2 C2004-901052-2

*Library of Congress Cataloging-in-Publication Data*
Rossiter, Sean, 1946–
 Hockey : how to play like the pros / Sean Rossiter & Paul Carson.
 p. cm
 Selections from the series Hockey the NHL Way.
 ISBN 1-55365–044-1 (trade paper : alk. paper)
 1. Hockey—Juvenile literature. I. Carson, Paul, 1955– II. Rossiter, Sean, 1946– Hockey the NHL Way. III. Title.
GV847.25.R65 2004
796.962—dc22 2004042543

Editing by Anne Rose
Cover design by Jessica Sullivan
Interior design by Peter Cocking
Instructional photographs: Stefan Schulhof/Schulhof Photography
Front cover photograph: Bruce Bennett/Bruce Bennett Studios
Printed and bound in Canada by Friesens
Printed on acid-free paper
Distributed in the U.S. by Publishers Group West

We gratefully acknowledge the financial support of the Canada Council for the Arts, the British Columbia Arts Council, and the Government of Canada through the Book Publishing Industry Development Program (BPIDP) for our publishing activities.

# CONTENTS

Powerful and fast, Mats Sundin is at home along the boards or in the slot. He can do the dirty work, make plays or finish around the net with his soft hands and scoring touch.

# Foreword

*Hockey the NHL Way: How to Play Like the Pros* teaches the skills any player age eight to 12 needs for a head start in the world's fastest sport. Seeing full-page action photographs—in colour—of National Hockey League stars such as Mike Modano, Scott Niedermayer, Martin Brodeur and Markus Naslund demonstrating the skills this book teaches will inspire young players to do the same.

I like to see young players who are learning the game try all the different positions so they can better understand all aspects of hockey. *Play Like the Pros* teaches the skills needed to play any position. The basics of teamwork, fair play and sportsmanship are here, too. You don't need a video or DVD player to learn from this book.

Hockey is as physical a game as any. As a player, you must make the game as safe as possible for everyone you share the rink with. That means keeping your stick down and your temper under control. It also means treating officials—and their decisions—with respect. Of all team sports, hockey is the one where players line up to shake hands with their opponents after important games. Sportsmanship is what makes this game of ours a thing of beauty.

The great game of hockey is more than just the elite players of the NHL. It's kids waking up early for practice, parents who get involved and coaches who give of their time and experience to help young people learn about hockey and life. Hockey means teamwork, dedication and friendships to remember—no matter how far you go in the game.

**Pat Quinn**
*Head Coach, The Toronto Maple Leafs*

"When I was 15 or 16, I worked on moving my feet as quick as I could. I think that helped. I always try to do that. It helps build both quickness and speed."

ADAM DEADMARSH

# FITNESS
## & PREPARATION

**IF YOU CAN'T SKATE**, you can't play hockey. That's why the best way to be a better hockey player is to become a better skater. And if you want to skate better, you need to be fit and strong.

NHL teams know this. So they hire fitness coaches to design individual off-ice workout programs for every player.

It's the same for you. The key to better skating is to build strength in your body's core and the muscles that radiate from there, such as the thighs. Increased strength enables you to adopt a lower stance on the ice, use your skateblade edges better and get full thrust from every power stroke. And remember: you don't need a rink to get stronger. Any old place will do.

A few simple pieces of exercise equipment can help you develop core strength, so that you will be more solid on your skates. If your team doesn't have this equipment, visit your local gym.

### Swiss ball

Many hockey players use the Swiss ball, a big plastic balloon, to help them do abdominal crunches. Use the Swiss ball to hold your legs up while you do crunches. Or lie face up on the ball, with your feet on the ground. Crunches develop the abdominal wall, which is a hockey player's strength platform.

### Balance board

For regular balance training, try using a balance board (a disc or rectangular platform mounted on a pivot). Just keeping the board

# Core strength

Doing crunches on a Swiss ball helps Kellin build his abdominal wall.

Standing on the balance board develops Michael's balance and agility.

Brad's ball toss starts with flexed elbows and knees, then he fully extends.

level while kneeling, sitting or standing will work your upper body, lower body and abdominal area. As your balance improves, you will be able to stay on the board longer.

### Medicine ball

A medicine ball, a heavy stuffed rubber ball, can improve your upper-body and abdominal strength. Pass the medicine ball back and forth with a partner using a two-handed chest pass. Remember to bend your knees and elbows when receiving a pass.

## Combinations

Use two or more pieces of equipment in the same exercise to get more from the activity. Combining various pieces of exercise equipment in different ways gives new life to old drills and can make them more effective. Do these off-ice exercises and you'll see direct payoffs on the ice: your muscles won't tire as quickly, and you'll stand taller and straighter, bend your knees deeper and longer and have better balance and agility.

## Swiss ball and medicine ball

Sit on a Swiss ball facing your partner and play catch with a medicine ball. Or sit back-to-back on Swiss balls set close together and hand the medicine ball off to one another: twist to your left to give, twist right to receive, and vice versa.

> **N H L   T I P**
> "Work on your core strength and your leg strength. That's where the Europeans can have such an advantage, because they are so strong in the lower body."
> **K E I T H   P R I M E A U**

New twist to the old sit-up: throwing a medicine ball from the Swiss ball crunch position.

Every part of Kellin's upper body works as he tosses the ball to a partner.

Ball catch on the balance board—a new Olympic sport?

## Core strength

## Balance board and medicine ball

Stand on a balance board and give and receive passes with a medicine ball. Squat in a deep knee bend, then find a good balance with your elbows tucked into your sides and your hands out in front, ready for the pass. A partner 6 feet/2 m in front of you passes the ball at chest level. As you catch it, try to stay balanced on the board. While your upper body is dealing with the medicine ball, your abdominal wall and legs are working hard to keep you balanced.

### Off-ice training

To add more speed and power to your game, you need strength. And that strength comes from dry-land training. In the off-season, you train to improve. During the hockey season, doing these exercises helps you maintain your fitness.

### Plyometrics

Jeremy Roenick does plyometrics. So do Simon Gagne and Ed Jovanovski. Plyometrics are jumping, hopping and bounding exercises that are good for on-ice quickness and agility. Young players can benefit from plyometric exercises too. But be careful. Plyometrics are high-risk exercises, so proper instruction is essential. Always try for a soft, stable landing and a quick reversal of direction.

# Building strength

Tara moves quickly in the opposite direction and "pops" her feet off the floor.

Bring your knees to your chest to clear the bench. Take off and land with knees bent.

Make sure the box is solid. Don't jump any higher than 18 inches/45 cm.

### Bounding exercises

Big, long, bounding strides work the muscles in your legs when you push off and when you land. You can bound forward or sideways, from the floor, a bench or a wooden horse.

- Balance on the balls of your feet with your knees bent.
- Push up, driving your arms forward to give you height. Bring your knees to your chest.
- Land on your entire foot when touching down to the side.

*Good for:* stride length and power.

## Deep squat jumps

Squat jumps develop leg strength.

- Squat with your weight on your heels, and your knees deeply bent.
- Push off from the balls of your feet by shifting your weight forward.
- Land lightly on your feet, bending your knees in one fluid motion.

*Good for:* low stance.

## Squat running and lunges

Squat running develops the quadriceps (the front of the thigh).

- Squat on the balls of your feet with your knees deeply bent. Place your hands behind your back, with one hand holding your opposite wrist.
- Run around the room, staying balanced in the squat position.

*Good for:* low stance.

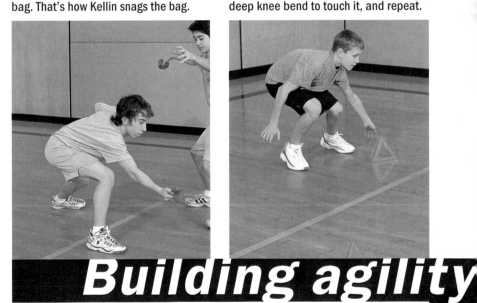

Lateral bounding: Start with a deep knee bend and do another between hurdles.

Front foot moves first, toward falling bean bag. That's how Kellin snags the bag.

Shuffle laterally to each pylon, do a deep knee bend to touch it, and repeat.

# Building agility

## Lateral running

Running from side to side imitates your skating drive stroke.

- Place 12 markers in two lines about 10 feet/3 m apart. Alternate the markers so that they make a zigzag pattern.
- Run to the first marker. As you turn to run to the next marker, plant your outside foot. Bend your knee deeply and push off to the next marker.
- Repeat with the remaining 11 markers.

*Good for:* stride length and power.

**Knee bends:** Stand with your arms at your sides, feet flat on the floor. Bend your knees. Hold for 45 seconds. *Good for:* calves.

**Calf stretch:** Stand facing the wall, one toe against the base-board, the other foot 3 feet/1 m behind facing forward. Lean your head and raised elbows against the wall. Switch legs. Hold for 45 seconds each leg. *Good for:* hamstrings (back of thigh), calves.

**Forward lunge:** Kneel on one knee, keeping your front leg ahead of your body. Extend your back leg as far behind you as it will go. Place your hands on the floor in line with your front foot to support you. Press down from the groin. Switch sides. Hold for 45 seconds each leg. *Good for:* hamstrings.

**Quad stretch:** Sit with one leg bent to the side. Touch your opposite foot to the bent leg's knee, using your arms behind your body

# Calves & hamstrings

Quad stretch. Lean gently back and forth to stretch your quadriceps and lower back.

Hamstring flexor. Reach for your ankle or your flexed foot, pulling your toes back for more calf stretch.

for support. Lean back to stretch one leg, then forward to stretch the other. Switch legs. Hold for 45 seconds each leg. *Good for:* quadriceps (front of the thigh), hips, lower back.

**Hamstring flexor:** Sit with one leg extended in front of you. Touch your opposite foot to the inner thigh of your extended leg. Lean forward, keeping your back straight. Switch sides. Hold for 45 seconds each leg. *Good for:* hamstrings, hips, lower back.

**Triceps stretch:** Stand with one arm behind your head, touching the top of your opposite shoulder blade. Hold the elbow of that arm with your opposite hand. Gently press down on your elbow, pushing your hand down your back. Switch arms. Hold for 10 seconds each arm. *Good for:* triceps, rotator cuffs (shoulder).

**Arm twist:** Stand with one arm behind your head, the other bent low behind your back. Start by touching the finger tips of each hand; work at grasping your knuckles. Switch arms. Hold for 5 seconds each arm. *Good for:* triceps, rotator cuffs.

**Triceps flexor:** Drop down on your hands and knees. Stretch one arm straight ahead of you on the floor. Grasp the elbow of your straight arm with your opposite hand. Lay your head on your bent arm. Press down on your elbow. Switch arms. Hold for 10 seconds each arm. *Good for:* triceps (back of the upper arm).

Triceps stretch: Press back with your head to add to the stretch.

Triceps flexor: Hold for 10 seconds each arm. Also good for your lower back muscles.

Hip flexor: Opening your hips will improve your upper-leg turnout for pivots.

# Shoulders & neck

**Forearm extension:** Drop down on your hands and knees. Turn your wrists so that your fingers point back toward your body. Lean back. Hold for 20 seconds. *Good for:* inner wrists.

**Neck stretch:** Lie on your back with your legs in front of you, knees up and bent. Grasp your hands behind your head. Lift your head straight up. Hold for 5 seconds. Work up to sets of three. *Good for:* neck, upper back.

**Hip flexor:** Sit with one leg extended in front of you. Bend your other leg toward you, holding the ankle in one hand and your toes in the other. Pull your foot toward your body until you feel a gentle stretch in the muscle. Don't force the stretch. Switch legs. Hold for 30 seconds each leg. *Good for:* groin, hips.

**Groin flexor:** Sit with your legs spread as wide as you can. Lean forward, keeping your back as straight as possible. Work toward touching the floor in front of you with your chest. Hold for 30 seconds. *Good for:* groin, hamstrings, lower back.

**Groin stretch:** Sit with your legs in front of you, knees bent and the soles of your feet touching. Hold your toes to keep your feet together. Lean forward, keeping your back as straight as possible. Hold for 45 seconds. *Good for:* groin (especially good for goalies).

# Back and hips

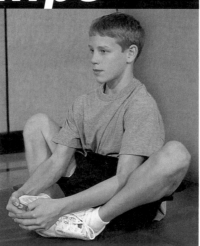

Groin flexor: Keep your back straight as you lean forward, toward the floor.

Groin stretch: Hold your soles together, pressing them to your body.

Torso twists: Try to get your crossover knee to the floor on the opposite side.

**Torso twists:** Lie on your back with your legs in front of you, knees up and bent. Cross one leg over the other at the knee. Grasp your hands behind your head. Keeping both shoulders on the floor, touch your crossover knee to the floor on the opposite side. Switch sides. Hold for 45 seconds each leg. *Good for:* glutes (bum), lower back.

**"Consistency is important: Stay in shape, work hard in practice and take a day off when needed. And try not to get too fired up when things don't go well."**

STEVE YZERMAN

Markus Naslund used his speed and pinpoint shot to finish second in the NHL scoring race two years in a row, 2002 and 2003.

# SKATING
## FOR POWER & SPEED

**U**NDERSTANDING HOW your skates work so that you use them better is the single best way to improve your game.

We will show you how the best skaters in the NHL use their quickness, agility and speed to make their other skills more deadly. We will show you how to add quickness for fast starts and changes of direction, and how to add straight-ahead speed by getting full-stride extension. After all, most stops in hockey are really just pauses before you rocket off somewhere else. We will show you how to skate hard, stop on a dime and make your getaway in a smooth series of steps.

We show you how. You supply the willpower—and the love of the game—that make it all possible.

**TO BEGIN**, you need to know the four simple steps you can take to improve your skating. Learning them is easy. Applying them to your skating style is the hard part. In the upcoming pages, we will put these four steps to use in each of the moves you make most often on the ice. The four steps are:

- **FIRST**: Get in shape. Skating the right way takes strength and flexibility.
- **SECOND**: Use a low, balanced stance on your skates. Bend your knees and ankles more.
- **THIRD**: Know where your skates are under your body, and use the edges of your skateblades.
- **FOURTH**: Fully extend your drive leg on every stride. Hip-knee-ankle-toe. Every time.

Apply these four key tips to each skating skill in this book, and you will take your biggest steps forward as a hockey player.

# Four steps to
# *better skating*

# agility & balance

**ONE WAY** that strength exercises pay off on the ice is by giving you better agility and balance on your skates. Control is the first step in adding speed and power to your skating.

Much of the game of hockey is played in small spaces. Being able to evade another player when you have the puck or stay with an opponent when checking requires agility.

Balance means being ready to move in any direction: to take hits, to pivot or turn with the play. Well-balanced skaters like Tony Amonte and Mats Sundin have their skates under their body mass and their upper bodies leaning forward but upright—even as their legs are pumping at top speed.

### Creating a solid base

Your stance makes everything else possible. If your stance is not right, your skating will not improve. To get into the right position, think of sitting in a chair:

- Bend your knees more. Seen from the side, your thighs should be almost horizontal.
- Line up your front knee at least a couple of inches ahead of the toe of your skate.
- Keep your back straight and hold your head up.

### How a lower stance works

A lower stance makes you solid on your skates. It puts your body mass over your front, or glide, skate. That improves your balance.

# Stance

Keith's ready position: deep knee bend, shoulders almost level, head up.

Almost like sitting, Keith's deep knee bend puts his knees ahead of his toes.

In motion: knees flexed, weight balanced, body extended, head up, arms reaching.

A deeper knee bend lets your power stroke drive farther back and to the side. And, with your body closer to the ice, you have a lower center of gravity. The lower you can get to the ice, the harder it will be for opponents to knock you off your feet.

With your back straight and your head up, you are balanced from side to side and from front to back. You are ready to see everything, go anywhere. Your first step could be in any direction.

Try this stance right now, where you are, without skates. It will feel awkward at first. Your thighs will start to hurt very soon. That pain tells you why you have to get stronger, and where.

## The power stroke

Once your body is lined up over your skates, the secret to staying balanced when skating is to keep your feet, as much as possible, right under your body mass. It's that simple. That's how you get the most power from every stroke.

When your power stroke is done, bring your drive skate—your back skate—quickly back under you, in line with your hip joint. At that moment you are totally balanced over your glide skate—your front skate.

Your recovering skate should come almost close enough to your glide skate to touch heels. Keep your glide leg in a deep knee bend while the drive leg fully extends. Recover, and you are balanced over your skates and ready to explode with another power stroke.

Practise by touching heels with every recovery.

Toe, knee, head all lined up, glide knee an inch or two/2.5 or 5 cm ahead of the toe.

As his drive skate recovers, Dylan pushes off his front inside edge.

After fully extending his drive skate, Keith shifts his weight to the glide skate.

# Body positioning

## Body positioning checklist

- Head, hips, glide knee and skate are in a straight line up-and-down, and balanced.
- Either way you look, front to back or side to side, the player is as balanced as possible.
- Feet are under the body and outside the hips only on the power stroke.

### Skating backward

Skating backward is easier than most people think. Just so you can feel better about trying it, start next to the boards. Grab the boards if you feel yourself falling.

Start skating backward by swinging one hip out and making a C-shaped cut in front and to the side as you move backward. Glide with the other foot. Continue to make C-cuts with each foot, one after another. You're skating backward!

Try to generate power by thrusting hard against the front inside edge of the skate you are making C-shaped cuts with.

It is important to begin practising backward skating by making sure you have a good base of support. Your feet should be hip-width apart, and your knees should be comfortably bent, in a

## Skating backward

Jordan swings his left hip and begins a C-cut with his left skate.

He finishes the C-cut and is already shifting weight to his right leg.

He is about to begin the right-side C-cut and is moving backward, under control.

**T I P**
As you try crossing over while gliding, remember to lean forward and into the turn for balance.

squat position. Your back should be straight with your head up and your eyes forward—a slight, forward lean will help you stay balanced.

### Skating tips

■ Keep low to the ice. Thrust hard with your back leg.
■ Your upper leg muscles should feel the strain. That's where power comes from.
■ When speed is what you want, carry your stick with your top hand alone.

# SKATING
## *control*

**WE ALL KNOW** what it's like to be out of control on skates. It's the first feeling we had on the ice.

The key to being in control at all times is being aware of your skateblade edges. For every movement you make on the ice, you use an edge. That's how you get where you want, when you want.

You can skate sideways, stop and go and do tight turns without striding—just by using your edges. You can also link those moves without stops or pauses along the way—just by using your edges.

When you're in control, you don't think, you just react. The game flows as the puck moves from player to player and team to team, and you flow with it. Less effort, more action.

## Check out your edges

There are inside and outside edges on your right and left skates, and because you skate both forward and backward, you use eight edges in total. If you are weak on one edge, you will lose control or fall.

## Using your edges

As you shift your weight forward, use the front part of the edge. Shifting your weight back puts you on the back half of your skate's edge. Leaning one way or another, or reaching out with your skate, brings an inner or outer edge into contact with the ice.

Most of the time, you use only one edge on each skate to stop or to change direction. If you are aware of your edges once you

# Edge control

Pay attention to your inside and outside edges as you practise any skating skill.

The lower body does the work, but twisting the upper body helps.

Edge control is the key to stopping, turning and moving sideways.

are in motion, slight shifts from side to side, forward or back can take you in a new direction or speed you up—all with very little effort, and without stopping or starting again.

## Weighting and unweighting

Often, to make quick changes in direction or spinning moves (called pivots), you lighten the weight on your skates by slightly straightening up from a bent-knee position. The word for this is "unweight." Unweight your skates and you can pivot faster.

## When to do a tight turn

The tight turn works like a U-turn on ice. Done right, you can come out of a tight turn faster than when you started into it. That makes it a good move for a puck carrier trying to shake off a checker. Paul Kariya is a master of the tight turn.

It is also a good way to react when the puck changes hands. When the play changes direction or reverses, a tight turn lets you stay in the action. Now you are speeding in the other direction, uncovered, either with the puck or ready to receive it.

## How to do it

Skate hard to where you want to make the turn. As you prepare to turn, step into it with your lead foot and hip, allowing your upper body to twist into the turn. Bend your knees and put your body

**T I P**

The tight turn is not exactly a U-turn. Do it right, and you leave more of a question mark on the ice—and on the face of your checker.

Making a sharp left turn, Tara sets it up with a deep knee bend.

She points her stick to the left, helping twist her upper body . . .

. . . which brings her out of the turn with more power. Note her deep knee bend.

# Tight turns

weight on the front part of your edges as you start the turn. Point your stickblade in the direction of your turn. Roll your wrists on your stick to help your upper body turn. Both feet point forward, positioning your inside skate just ahead of your outside one. Keep your weight over the middle of your skates.

Weight the back outside edge of your lead skate—the inside skate—to finish. Drive off the back inside edge of your outside skate to power away. Cross over with your outside leg to finish the turn.

### When to do a crossover

After the forward stride, the next most important basic skating skill is the forward crossover. You probably already know how to do it, but here's how to do a better, faster crossover.

Done right, a crossover can help you add speed as you move to one side or the other.

The difference is more power from a lower stance, and twice the push by your full extension of both legs. You are getting two pushes instead of one.

### How to do it

As you skate forward, keep your knees bent deep. Weight the front outside edge of your inside skate and the front inside edge of your outside skate after you cross. Carry your stick in both hands with the blade on or near the ice in front of your body.

# Crossovers

Push hard with your inside foot as you step over it with your outside foot.

With the crossover complete, Luke is ready to push off his inside edge.

Pushing off the front outside edge of your crossover foot adds power and speed.

**T I P**

Lean into the turn when you do a crossover. Hold your stick with both hands close together, and keep the stickblade on the ice.

Then, push to the side hard and under on the front outside edge of your inside skate, as you transfer your weight and cross your outside skate over your inside one. Keep your crossover skate low.

Use the front inside edge of your crossover foot to bite into the ice as you shift your weight over that foot. Push back and to the side as you fully extend your crossover leg.

As your skate reaches its fullest extension, step to the inside with your inside foot.

## When to do a crossunder

This move is actually much simpler than the forward crossover. It only seems difficult when you're not yet comfortable skating backward.

As a defender, you can use a crossunder to add speed while checking an opposing puck carrier, usually in the defensive zone. And as you skate backward, you can also control the gap between you and the puck carrier, and move sideways faster. Even if you're not a defenseman, remember that when your team doesn't have the puck, each skater is a defender.

## How to do it

Skating backward with your knees bent, your outside foot rarely leaves the ice. It forms C-cuts to add power to each step. Keep your weight over that outside foot.

Fully extend your crossunder foot to add more power to your stride.

Tara shows good leg reach, pulling from the front inside edge of her inside foot . . .

. . . and finishing her stride by fully extending the leg that crosses under her body.

# *Crossunders*

To begin, step with your inside leg out wide, reaching as far as possible. Grip the ice with the front inside edge of your inside skate and pull that skate under your body. Shift from the inside edge to the front outside edge of that same skate and drive hard, fully extending your leg. Reach inward again with the inside skate, grip the ice, and repeat.

Most players find doing crossunders easier one way than the other. Work on doing them both ways.

### Why pivot?

In the flow of a game the puck changes hands hundreds of times. You switch from offense to defense and back again several times each shift. Some athletes play only offensive or defensive roles. But hockey players have to do both, and sometimes that change means going from forward to backward skating, and back again, in split-seconds.

### Forward-to-backward pivot

This pivot is also called the "Mohawk turn." You can use it when your team loses the puck and you are caught behind the play. Skate hard into your team's zone, then pivot from forward to backward skating, staying between your check and the goal.

# Pivots

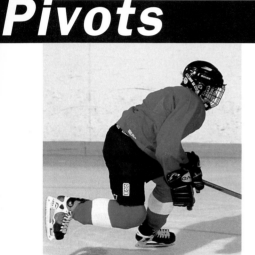

Skate hard, glide, then turn on the front inside edge of your lead skate.

Luke has transferred his weight to his opposite skate . . .

. . . now he moves backward, weight balanced, doing a C-cut with his left skate.

### How to do it

Start by skating hard, then deepen your knee bend and glide on one skate. Shift your weight over your glide skate and begin opening your hip on the side you want to turn to. Turn your knee and your skate in the direction you want to go. Turn your head and shoulder that way, too. With your heels together and your toes out, turn on the front inside edge of your glide skate. Shift your weight from your glide skate to the one pointing backward.

SKATING

# *quickness*

**PASSING, CHECKING AND BATTLING** for the puck usually take place within small areas of the ice, where winning these mini-battles is more important than sheer end-to-end speed. Your first step is all-important. Moving in the right direction with that first step is the key.

Think about how most goals are scored. Few are scored off the rush. More often, a series of defensive mistakes leads to a score. Most goals come off turnovers.

To take advantage of those mistakes, you need to read the play, anticipate the action and react to the sudden change of possession. If you are near a loose puck, you have to move fast to get control of it. If you are away from the puck, go to the nearest open space. Remember . . . your first quick step is the key.

### When to stop

Often the first thing to do when the puck changes hands is to stop on a dime. Stopping can be the quickest way to change direction because you don't even have to come to a full stop. A one-foot stop and crossover can get you moving in a new direction faster than a quick turn.

A quick stop is also a way to shake a checker and protect the puck. Cross the offensive blueline at top speed and, if your way to the net is blocked, stop dead in your tracks. Make sure your checker hasn't stopped, too. Then look for a pass receiver in the middle. If your teammates are covered, or you can see no pass, get the puck deep into the zone along the boards.

# Stops and starts

Hands on stick for balance, Keith stops on the outside edge of his inside skate.

Looking in the direction he wants to go, he crosses over with the other skate . . .

. . . and gets going with short, choppy strides on his front inside edges.

### One-foot stop and half-turn

With both hands on your stick for balance, turn to one side, lean back, flex your knees and drive the front outside edge of your inside—or trailing—skate into the ice.

Look back in the direction you came from. Your front skate will be off the ice as you stop. Cross it over the skate you stopped with and drive hard off the skate that's still on the ice. Let go of your stick with your lower hand.

Start taking choppy steps with the front inside edge of your crossover skate, driving your arms forward to add power to your strides.

## Hockey stop

This is a two-footed stop. Use it when you have no choice but to come to a halt.

It's a good idea to have your stickblade on the ice when doing the hockey stop. It makes a third point of contact with the ice. Most players stop better one way than the other. Often it will seem easier when you're turned to the side you shoot from. Work on stopping both ways.

## How to do it

As you turn sideways to stop, the heel of one skate should be level with the toe of the other. Your trailing skate should be slightly ahead. Hold your stick in both hands, and keep your stickblade close to the ice when you stop.

### TIP

Don't be afraid to fall when you are working on stops and starts. The ice is slippery. Everybody falls. The trick is in how fast you get up again.

Turned sideways, Jaysen comes into the stop with his knees almost straight.

He digs his edges into the ice and bends his knees to add more stopping power.

He sees the pass—his stop allowed him to shake his check.

## Hockey stop

Relax your knee bend going into the stop. That helps unweight your skates.

Now drive the front inside edge of your front skate and the front outside edge of your back skate into the ice. Flex your knees, using them as shock absorbers to get more force and stopping power as your edges cut into the ice.

Don't just stop. Stop, then read and react.

If you're stopping to lose your check and you are open, have your stickblade on the ice. Look for the pass.

### Get going

There's no point in stopping just to stand around and watch the game. You want to get going again right away.

Always try to convert your straight-ahead energy into a turn, so you can go in another direction. If you can't do that, sometimes you need to set out from a standing start.

### V-start

Use the V-start to get going from a standing position when you need a fast, explosive burst of energy.

### How to do it

Balance your weight on the front inside edges of your skates—heels close together, toes out. Your knees are about shoulder-width apart, deeply flexed and bent outward.

# Explosive starts

Skates forming a V, stick in one hand, Derek drives off his front inside edge.

Up to five choppy strides later, he starts to fully extend his strides.

By the time he makes the blueline, Derek shows good drive-skate recovery.

### T I P
Try not to rush around all the time. Keep a little bit in the tank so you can explode into a higher gear when you see the right opening.

Explode from this V-stance with three to five choppy strides, staying on the front inside edges of your skates. Take small, quick, choppy steps.

Lead with your chest. Keep your head up. Hold your stick with your top hand, driving your arms front to back to add power to your straight-ahead speed.

After three to five short steps, start to extend your strides, then begin fully extending your drive leg to build speed.

## Crossover starts

This move gets you going sideways. Use it after a two-foot stop, with one crossover step leading to a V-start.

You can do a crossover start while skating either backward or forward. It is used most often by defensemen to block the way of a puck carrier.

But it can be a great move to get around a defenseman when you have the puck. Joe Sakic looks like a freight train coming in on a defenseman, he then moves just as fast to the side, getting himself open to take a shot.

## How to do it

From a stop position, turn your head and shoulders in the direction you want to go. Keep your head up and your shoulders level. It also helps to point your stick in the direction you're going in.

**T I P**
When you master the crossover start, learn to do it without looking where you are going. It can be a puck carrier's secret weapon.

In the ready position you are balanced on the outside edge of your inside blade.

Turning his upper body shifts Brad's weight to his inside leg.

His outside leg crosses over. He drives off the left front outside edge to gain speed.

# Crossover starts

Cross over with your outside leg, keeping your crossover knee low for good balance. You want to just clear your stationary skate.

After you cross over, reach sideways in the direction you want to go with the skate on that side. Grip the ice with the front inside edge, and pull inwards. After the first crossover step, twist your body into the V-start position for two or three more short, quick strides. Keep your head up and on a swivel. A sudden sideways move can put you in traffic.

**POWER IS ENERGY** in motion. In hockey that means movement, and skating is one of the fastest ways a human can move.

In skating, you get power from your stride leg, which adds to both speed and balance. You need power to fight your way along the boards or keep your place in front of the net. You have to keep your legs moving when sticks and bodies are holding you up.

That takes strength. It takes strength to keep a deep stance and get the most out of your skating stride and extension. But it is worth the effort. When strength and proper skating form come together, one result is more speed. And the need for speed is greatest in the fastest game on two feet.

# *power*
SKATING

## How balance leads to power

Power is hard to see, but it's like a coiled spring that releases energy as it unwinds. If you can control how much energy you release, and in what direction, you will be a controlled, powerful skater.

One reason great skaters like Mario Lemieux and Teemu Selanne make it look so easy is that their upper bodies barely move—even when they are skating at top speed. When you are balanced over your skates, you can focus all of your energy in one direction—straight ahead—without losing any speed to side-to-side wobbles.

The secret is to have your body weight balanced over your skates as much as possible. Your body has to be centered over

### T I P

By keeping your head still even as you skate at top speed, you can see around you better. Your head swivels easier when it is not moving from side to side.

At the moment of stride recovery, Lance has both feet under him.

Lance starts into a good low recovery. His head is lined up over his glide skate.

Even with full extension, Kellin's upper body and head are perfectly balanced.

## Stability

your glide skate when you recover from your power stroke. This shift in weight over your glide skate prepares that leg for the next power stroke, and that puts the mass of your body behind the power stroke. After each full extension of the drive leg, recover as low to the ice as you can to get your other leg's power stroke off to a quicker start.

### Power checklist

- Keep your head up, your eyes forward and your upper body still.
- Drive your arms straight ahead to propel yourself forward.
- Keep your body mass over your edges for better balance.

### Hip-knee-ankle-toe

Some of the fastest players in the NHL, like Scott Niedermayer, seem to glide around the ice, hardly working at all. Once your stance is balanced, the key to more speed is your power stroke. Think of each big joint—hip-knee-ankle-toe—as adding more power to your stroke.

### How to do it

Your power stroke should be out to the side and back. It has to be outward for you to get the most out of your front inside edge. It has to be behind you to push your glide skate forward.

Feel it happen. Your power stroke should start at the hip, driving your biggest leg muscles out and back. Next, you

# Full extension

Both feet are under Luke's body. His drive foot is ready to uncoil.

That final toe flick gives one last shot of power. Head, knee, foot, all lined up.

Seen from the front, Luke's extension causes a slight weight shift to that side.

> ### N H L   T I P
> "When you get to your top speed, stride out as far as you can. Let your body relax. Nice and slow and long strides."
> **T O N Y   A M O N T E**

straighten your knee. Then you extend your foot at the ankle. A final toe flick completes the stroke.

It takes more time to do all those things right. That's what makes skating the right way look easy. Your power stroke is slower, your legs are pumping less, but you are skating faster.

Listen to your skates on the ice when you get full extension. They sound different. There's a raspy *snick!* at the end of the stroke. It's that toe flick biting into the ice.

That's the way to make the most of your strength. You need to convert all the strength you have to speed.

Hart and Norris Trophy–winner Chris Pronger's full extension and balance, seen here as he beats a checker, give him power and surprising speed for a big man.

"Finding openings to shoot from is a mental skill. You have to be able to read the play." Getting to those openings in time takes quickness.

ZIGGY PALFFY

# SCORING

## SECRETS

**G**OAL SCORERS don't get enough credit. Oh yeah? It's the goal scorers who get all the glory, right? True. But they still don't get enough respect, because many people think goal scorers are born with a gift, while some think they can do only one thing. But here's the secret. Goal scorers know the game of hockey from the inside out.

Look for yourself. Goal scorers don't follow the puck, the puck finds their sticks. A goal scorer sees more, knows more and is more aware. The moves are automatic. That comes from watching the game closely, from trying different moves, fiddling with sticks, imagining new ways to play and checking out the other team's goalie during warmups.

So work on being a goal scorer yourself. Be a student of the game.

"There are nights when you don't feel that great, but you have to be able to suck it up and play for your teammates. You have to sacrifice yourself every night."

MARK RECCHI

Why do many hockey players wind up, hammer the puck and then miss the net? Good question. Maybe they like the noise the puck makes when it hits the glass. Or maybe it's because only great goal scorers follow these six rules—all the time.

## 1. Be ready

If you are anywhere near the net, carry the puck in the shooting or ready position. Your first option is always to shoot, so carry the puck to the net in the ready position. Then you can shoot at any time, off either foot.

## 2. Shoot quick

Shooting quickly is more important than shooting hard. It's not the fastest shot that scores if the goalie is ready to stop it.

> ### N H L   T I P
> "My most effective way to score is to use my speed and anticipation to get into openings and then release the puck as quickly as I can on net."
> **P A U L   K A R I Y A**

Always carry the puck in the shooting position if you're anywhere near the net.

Don't wait while you decide where to shoot. Scorers shoot quickly...

. . . and they get the puck on the net. You never know, it might go in.

# Scoring secrets

But a quick shot takes a goalie by surprise, as Jason Arnott can tell you. "You have to get your shot off quickly because goalies are so good in the NHL, and, often, a quick shot is more successful."

## 3. Shoot on the net

Why would you do anything else? Simple. Some players only want to score on the perfect shot: top shelf, both posts and in, off the scoreboard, nothing but net. But you don't get points for style in this game. Make it easy on yourself. Hit the net.

### 4. Shoot low

Shoot low, unless you are in close and the goalie is down. A goalie's hands are quicker than his or her feet. Low shots produce more rebounds. Patrick Roy knows most of the goals scored against him came along the ice, which is why so many goalies play the butterfly style. But a butterfly goalie has to get down and back up. Any time you can catch the goalie moving—up or down on the ice, in or out of the net—shoot low.

### 5. Know the goaltender's weaknesses

Look for openings and shoot where you see the net. Look five-hole then low stick-side. Goalies will tell you how to score on them—if you watch. Does the stick come off the ice when the goalie moves

# Scoring secrets

Shoot low. Brandon is moving sideways, opening the five-hole, but Jordan crosses in front and scores on the goalie's stick side.

Think save and expect rebounds. Pull the puck back and go upstairs.

sideways? Is the glove hand high or low? Do you see a five-hole? How does the goalie handle being scored on? Those are some of the ways goalies tell you what to do.

### 6. Expect rebounds

Be at the net when your teammates shoot and have your stickblade on the ice. Let's face it: not all of your team's shots are going to go in. Go where you think the puck will be after the goalie makes the save. If it goes in, what did you lose? If not, make the second shot count. Or the third.

# *stick work*

**LEARNING DOESN'T** make you smart. It makes you educated. Developing hockey skills won't always make you a star, either, but it will make you a better hockey player. It will teach you that you can learn with your body, just as you learn with your mind.

You already do many things without thinking. Spelling common words, for example, or doing simple math problems in your head. It's the same with hockey. Skills that are awkward at first become smooth and effortless if you do them often enough.

This chapter will help you play better with the puck. And once you stop thinking about stickhandling and deking, you can think about other things—like what you'll do when you get to the net.

If you can't receive the puck, and carry and protect it from your opponents, you can't play hockey. Luckily, good stickhandlers are not born, they're made. And you *can* make yourself a magician with the puck. All you need to do is practise the tips and drills in this section.

### Check your stick

Usually, the first step to improving your stickhandling is to shorten your stick. Your stick is your main tool for handling the puck. In order to make a tight turn away from your shooting side, you need to be able to move your top hand across in front of your body with your stickblade flat on the ice. Is your stick short enough to do that?

# *Stickhandling*

Tyler shows proper puck-carrying stance: knees flexed, hands relaxed, head up.

Gloves off, we can see him grip the stick with his fingers, not his palms.

You get a better feel by cupping the puck with the toe of your stick.

**T I P**
Practise stickhandling without your gloves, so you can see yourself using your wrists.

### In good hands

A good stickhandler uses a short grip, with hands close together (8–12 inches/20–30 cm apart) at the top of the stick.

Roll your wrists to handle the puck. One way to make sure you use your wrists is to keep your elbows away from your body. Don't squeeze your stick. Use an easy grip, mostly with your fingers.

You can control the puck best with the middle-to-toe areas of your stickblade. That's where your wrist movements have the greatest effect. That's where you have the most feel.

Practising stickhandling drills 〔...〕 a smooth, tricky, puck-control artist. The drills in 〔...〕 developed by Dave King, an NHL and Canadia〔...〕 coach. They can be done at the rink or on any other 〔...〕e.

## Practise on your own

■ Stand with one foot on each side of a line 〔...〕on using your wrists, and make quick, neat sweeps. 〔...〕 row and wide sweeps. Do the same with only your top hand, then your bottom hand. Next, move the puck back and forth, but lift your stick 12 inches/30 cm or so between sweeps. Do narrow and wide sweeps, but always lift your stick. This drill will prepare you for handling the puck when your opponents' sticks are nearby.

> **T I P**
> Practise stickhandling with a puck and the toe of your stickblade pointed down, with a bladeless stick or with the butt end of your stick.

Side to side across the line. Quick movements.

Jesse rolls his wrists and keeps his elbows out as he does figure-8s.

Weight shift from foot to foot, hands 12 inches/30 cm apart. Cup the puck.

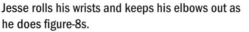

# *Stickhandling drills*

■ Add footwork. Place your gloves on the ice 3 feet/90 cm apart. Move the puck in a figure-8 around the gloves, both ways. Move your feet when you have to but stay square to the gloves. After a few sessions, start moving your head: up, down, side to side. Use the toe of your blade.

■ Now set your gloves 6 feet/1.8 m apart. Move your feet so you go from side to side while doing a figure-8 with the puck. Use a T-push to move sideways. Remember: To make the forehand move, your top hand must cross in front of your body.

Stickhandling your way through an opposing team is one of the great thrills of hockey. It requires the ability to control the puck with your stick and skates, as well as a skill known as "deking."

Stickhandling is the way you handle the puck and carry it with you. The first thing you'll notice when you're handling the puck in a game is that you attract checkers. Deking is what you do to get past them.

There are many ways to deke. You can go from forehand to backhand, or vice versa. But all dekes have some kind of fake as part of the move, and work best when completed at full speed. In fact, just speeding up at the right time is a deke in itself.

The term "deke" comes from "decoy." A decoy is used to draw someone or something into a trap. *Your* bait is the puck. You hold it out to an opponent; when the checker goes for it, you take

# Deking

Here the puck carrier dekes toward the boards, then moves the puck between the checker's stick and skates . . .

. . . then he bursts past, picking up the puck and skating hard.

it back and speed on past. The idea, of course, is to be tricky. Coach Dave King calls deking the most creative part of hockey.

One common type of deke is to move the puck through the triangle formed by an opponent's stickblade and toes, then move quickly to pick up the puck and skate around the checker. Add a head fake away from the direction you intend to go, then move the puck through the checker's stick and skates. The drills in this section focus on this type of deke.

SCORING

# *passing*

**PASSING IS** what makes hockey a team game. When you play as a team against six individuals who happen to be wearing the same jerseys, you should win every time. Why? Because the right pass beats more than one checker. Two or three good passes will put the puck at your opponents' doorstep.

When you have the puck, remember: you have four teammates you can pass it to. When your team has the puck but you don't, your job is to get free for a pass.

Passing is one of the easiest skills to practise and improve at. Receiving passes is usually more difficult. So work on becoming a dependable receiver. If your teammates know you'll make the effort, you'll see a lot more of the puck.

There are four basic passes in hockey. In each case, make sure that you:

- keep both hands away from your body, so that your stickblade stays square to the target until the follow-through, and
- cup the puck with your stickblade.

If you find your top hand is tight against your body, your stick may be too long or the lie may be incorrect.

### The forehand pass

This is the easiest pass to make: a simple sweep of the stick toward the target. If your receiver is moving, remember to aim the puck well ahead of the receiver's stick, not their body. Bring the puck back to your back foot, release at the front foot. Follow through low, pointing your stickblade at the target.

# Making passes

Jesse has his eye on his teammate, his stick cupping the puck . . . and his top hand away from his body. His hands work as a unit.

He follows through, shifting his weight and pointing his stick at the target.

### The backhand pass

This pass is used when you want to get the puck to someone on your backhand side. Sight your target out of the corner of your eye. Try to keep your lower shoulder down, so your stickblade— and the puck—stay on the ice. Again, hands move together. The motion of a backhand pass causes your upper body to twist and your lower shoulder and hand to rise, making it easier to raise the puck. Follow through low. Stickblade square to the target.

## The flip pass

To avoid sticks or bodies on the ice between you and your receiver, use a flip pass. Use your wrists to draw the puck toward yourself, then snap your stickblade up and under the puck. But don't overdo it. This is a pass, not a shot. Remember, the puck must land flat on the ice before it reaches the target.

## The drop pass

This is the quickest way to move the puck between teammates, and often results in an unchecked puck carrier. The passer simply stops the puck and leaves it for the trailing teammate. But beware. Make sure that the player behind you is your teammate. If the player isn't, your opponents are off on a breakaway—and you are going in the wrong direction.

**Backhand pass:** upper hand away from the body, front shoulder down. Cup the puck.

Smooth follow-through. Weight on the front foot, point the stick at the target. Look where the pass is going.

# Making passes

## Passing checklist

- The right pass is usually the easy pass. The longer the pass, the less likely the puck will get there.
- Hands work together, not against each other. Keep your stickblade square to the target.
- If you are the puck carrier, try to make eye contact with your receiver. Many passes don't click because the receiver has no idea they are coming.

A pass that is not received loses your team the puck most of the time. The next time you watch a game, count the number of passes tried but not received. Even in the NHL, too many players give up on passes that are not perfect.

Receiving passes is more difficult than making them. Practise receiving bad passes. Passes behind you, passes into your skates, passes coming from behind, passes that arrive in the air—all are chances to show how much you want the puck.

**If the pass is off-target:** Reach for the pass by dropping your bottom hand off your stick. This will extend your reach. Just stop the puck with your stick held by your top hand, then go after it.

**If the pass is behind you:** There are two things you can do. You can stop. Or you can reach back with your top hand on the stick and your stickblade angled so the puck will rebound up to your back skate. Kick the puck up to your stick, which you are now holding with both hands.

# Receiving passes

Bad pass. Will lets go of the stick with his bottom hand and reaches with his top hand only. Front knee bends deep to give him better reach.

The puck will deflect ahead off Will's back skateblade to his stick.

***TIP***

To improve your pass receiving, get your elbows up as the puck gets close. This helps you get your entire stickblade on the ice.

**If the pass is into your skates:** Angle your skate on the side the pass is coming from, toe in, and deflect the puck up to your stick. Or, if the pass is coming further back, put one foot behind the other, creating a 2-foot/61-cm-long target for the puck to hit. Shorten up on your stick to control the puck better when it arrives.

**If the pass is off the ice:** Try to catch the pass without closing your hand on the puck. Just stop the puck with your open palm, drop it in front of you and play the puck with both hands on your stick. Don't wave your stick at high passes.

## Pass receiving checklist

- The trick to receiving passes is to be available. When your team has the puck, look for open ice.
- Think "catching," not "stopping," the puck when you receive a pass. Relax your grip. Reach toward the puck and absorb its impact.
- Part of being available for a pass is making it easy for the passer. Be visible. Try to skate across the passer's field of vision in the neutral zone. Hold your stick on the ice as a target.
- Sometimes the long way around is the shortest route to receiving the puck. By skating in a semicircle to a spot not

> **N H L   T I P**
> "The key to receiving a bad pass is to use your entire body. Practise taking pucks off your skates and using your stick to knock down passes in the air."
> **P A U L   K A R I Y A**

Jordan reaches back for a pass behind him. His stick deflects the puck toward him . . .

. . . and he kicks it up with his back foot . . .

. . . to his stickblade, angled inward to receive the puck. This requires practise.

# *Receiving passes*

far away, you can be at full speed when the puck comes, and in a better position to see it coming.
- Receive a bouncing puck with your skate behind your stick-blade. Don't lift your stick off the ice. Back it up with your foot.
- Don't give up on bad passes. The more often you convert bad passes to completed passes, the more you'll get the puck.

**THE DIFFERENCE** between scorers and everybody else is not skill level. The difference is that top scorers think differently. They know they can score. They know they can score from anywhere near the net. They know that even if the goalie makes the save there will be a rebound, and they go after that rebound.

Great scorers know that if they don't score this time, they will the next time. And you know what? So can you. Any decent hockey player can be a goal scorer. It helps to be able to receive, carry and protect the puck—these are the basic skills, and some goal scorers don't have them all. But if you want to score goals, the skill you need most is the ability to shoot the puck accurately. This chapter shows you how.

# *shooting*

## SCORING

"One of the keys to coming back from an injury is proper rehabilitation and conditioning. And remember to stay positive."

GARY ROBERTS

The wrist shot is an all-purpose, hard, accurate shot. It can be used when you are standing still or skating fast.

## How to do it

**Body position**: Try to stay relaxed. Cup the puck with the middle of your stickblade. Feel it there. Keep your eyes on the target.

**The shot:** Sweep your stick forward. Just as it passes your body, bend both wrists back. Then snap them closed. The upper wrist pulls back on the top of your stick. The lower wrist supplies power and determines how high the shot will go.

**Follow-through:** Shift your weight to your front skate and follow through, aiming your stickblade at the target. To keep your shot low, follow through with your lower wrist on top of your stick and the toe of your stick pointing at your target.

# The wrist shot

A textbook wrist shot starts with the puck well back...

...Jesse's power stroke is bending his stick as he lets the shot go...

...and follows through, pointing his stickblade at the target and rolling his bottom wrist over.

## Wrist shot checklist

- Use both wrists. Turn both wrists open, then snap both closed at the moment of release. Feel your upper thumb pull the top of your stick toward your body.
- Shift weight from your back to front skate for power.
- Turn your body into the shot.
- Follow through, pointing your stickblade at your target, at the height you want. Feel your lower thumb curl around your stick to keep the shot low.

The closest thing to a secret weapon in hockey is the backhand shot. Vincent Damphousse uses it. Adam Oates uses a straight, shortened stickblade to improve his. And Mark Messier uses it more than any player in the NHL. Curved sticks have almost eliminated the backhand shot from the game, so goalies don't expect it. The backhand motion tells goalies to expect the puck to go high. Shooters who can keep their backhand shots down can score a lot of goals.

## How to do it

The backhand shot is done exactly the same way as the wrist shot, but from the other side of your body. Use the same sweeping motion with your stick, the same wrist snap, the same weight transfer from skate to skate and the same follow-through.

Jordan sneaks a peek at his target from the corner of his eye.

Power comes from upper body uncoiling and weight shift.

Keep it smooth. Keep the shot low by following through low.

## The backhand shot

**Body position:** Concentrate on dropping your front shoulder to get the stickblade flat on the ice.
**Follow-through:** A low follow-through keeps your backhand low.

## Backhand checklist

- Just do it. Half the battle is trying the backhand shot.
- Get your body into it. Start with your front (lower) shoulder down. Keep your upper hand in close.
- Don't flip the puck, drive it. Follow through low.

## How to do it

You should wait to work on your slap shot. It is hard on you, hard on your stick and hard to control, and the windup takes time. But who wants to wait? What a feeling you get! What power! What a noise! So if you're going to practise it, you might as well do it right.

**Body position:** The puck is opposite your front foot. Look at the puck, not the target. Keep your head down all the way.

**Hands:** Grip your stick firmly with your top hand. Slide your lower hand down the shaft as you reach back, then lock that hand.

**The shot:** Your weight will shift naturally to your front foot as you swing. Feel the entire force of your arms and shoulders behind the shot as your weight moves forward. Your stickblade should hit the ice just behind the puck, which you want to hit near the heel. Snap your wrists at the moment of impact.

# The slap shot

Eyes on the puck. Breathe in. Keep your backswing low to get the shot off faster.

Get your body into it. Contact the ice a couple of inches behind the puck.

Continue the body twist. All weight on your front skate. Aim at the target.

**Follow-through:** Follow through as far as you want. Keep all your weight on your front foot as you swing your stickblade at the target. How high a slap shot goes depends on where in your swing you hit the puck—the further forward you hit it, the higher it will go.

## Slap shot checklist

- Where is the puck? Look.
- Keep your head down until you follow through.
- Hit the ice a few inches/centimetres behind the puck.

The snap shot is the quickest shot you can get away, and it's one of the toughest shots for a goalie to stop. You can also shoot from close to your feet, so there is almost no windup and no warning. It is a combination wrist and slap shot.

A crisp snap shot gives you the element of surprise—by enabling you to shoot from a crowd. It is tough to master but very rewarding.

## How to do it

The snap shot takes more practise than other shots. Work on shooting off all the points along a tight quarter-circle, running from your forehand side next to your front foot to right in front of your feet with your front foot pointed out. Breathe out hard on the power stroke to add explosiveness.

**T I P**
Bend your knees on the follow-through to keep your balance.

Michelle's weight is on her inside leg all the way.

The shot is released in front of the feet, before the goalie is ready.

Her body twists to add power. This is a classic snap shot.

# The snap shot

**Body position:** The puck can be anywhere on your forehand side, even in front of you. You can be moving sideways across the goalmouth. It's also a great one-timer shot off a pass.
**Hands:** Bring your stickblade back on the ice. Keep your wrists cocked on the power stroke and your follow-through short. Contact point: middle of the blade. Stroke: short, but explosive.
**Follow-through:** Keep your balance; many players fall backward after the forward weight transfer. The rear foot often leaves the ice during the follow-through, so be aware of checkers nearby.

Most goals are scored from within the "shooting zone"—an imaginary triangle on the ice from which most of the goalmouth can be seen. From here, you are close enough to the goal to beat the goalie with a good shot.

If you are in your opponents' shooting zone, you should almost always shoot the puck. Why not pass? Because the shooting zone is a busy place. A pass in the zone usually ends up on an opponent's stick, or sometimes your teammate will lose the puck. Pass *into* the shooting zone, but not from *inside* it.

### The passing moment

The one time you *should* pass in the shooting zone is on a two-on-one—*if* you are 100 per cent sure you can get the puck past

# The shooting zone

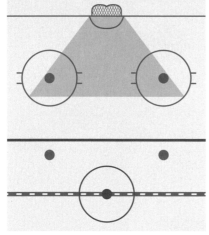

If you have the puck inside this triangle, shoot. Your teammate takes the rebound.

Here, Will's teammate, Tyler, is outside the shooting zone. *Never* pass from the slot. Tyler should go to the net.

the defender. But always move the puck hard to the net and look as if you mean to shoot. Carry the puck in the ready position—on your shooting side. That's how to make the goalie commit to you, leaving your teammate for the easy tap-in.

Remember: If you have the puck in the shooting zone, you have a good chance to score. If you lose the puck, you lose that chance. Passing inside the shooting zone often loses the puck for your team. So shoot. Put the puck on the net, then go to the net. Think rebound.

SCORING

# *deke or shoot?*

**FINALLY. IT'S YOU** and the goalie. You've imagined this
moment dozens of times. What do you do? The goalie
will tell you. Not by talking, but by showing you how he or
she is playing. It's called "body language." It's not hard
to figure out. All you have to do is look.

Is the goalie in or out of the net? No matter how the
goalie is playing, there are several options you can use.
Read and react.

Scoring is a numbers game. Not the number of goals
and assists you rack up, but the options you have each
time you're in scoring position. There is always more
than one way to score. It's your choice. See what the
goalie is giving you, and take it.

Always remember: You have the puck. That gives
you the edge.

When you are in the shooting position, you carry the puck to one side. That means the puck has a different view of the net and the goalie than you do. This is called the "shooter's illusion."

There are two differences between what you see and what the puck sees. First, the puck is on the ice while your eyes are well above it. Second, the puck is almost the length of your stick away from you. The difference between what you see and what the puck sees can work for or against you. You want to make this illusion work for you.

### In front

Say you are directly in front of the net, with the puck on your stick, forehand side. The goalie, too, is standing exactly in the middle of the goalmouth. You see the same amount of net on both sides of the goalie. But the puck sees more net than you do. So you shoot.

# The shooter's illusion

The goalie is lined up with the shooter, not the puck. Go short side.

The goalie is playing her angle perfectly. There's very little to shoot at.

Coming from your proper wing, the puck sees more net on the short side.

### On your wing

It works even better from an angle. Say you shoot left—most right-handers do—and you are on your proper wing, between the faceoff dot to the left of the net and the goal crease. The goalie, once again, is midway between the posts as you see them. But the puck sees more net on the short side. If you see net there, shoot to that side. Go for the rebound.

## The off-wing

Here's where the shooter's illusion works best of all. You are on your off-wing, the right side. Same situation: goalie centred. The puck sees more net on the far, or long, side. And the closer you get to the net, the more net the puck sees. So get closer and shoot for the far side.

You won't see the opening, but the puck will. *You* might not even see it go into the net.

## If the goalie is playing the angles right

Don't be fooled. Goalies learn about the shooter's illusion the hard way. A goalie playing the angles correctly lines up with the puck, not your body. When this happens, in the examples above you will see more net on the short side. But that is the same illusion working for the goalie. It's called "playing the angles."

> **T I P**
> Check whether the goalie is lined up with the puck *or* your body. If the goalie is centred between the posts, you have the edge. Take your best shot.

Here's one way the shooter's illusion can work for the goalie. You see lots of net up high . . .

. . . but the puck, down on the ice, sees very little net. Brandon has everything covered.

# The shooter's illusion

## Shooter's illusion checklist

- On a breakaway, start giving yourself the edge by moving a bit to one side or the other. Make the goalie react.
- If the goalie doesn't move, shoot the puck. Most of the time, you'll hit nothing but net.
- The closer you are to the net, the more net the puck will see. Move in closer.

"When I get a breakaway, I have a couple of moves in mind. It depends on the goalie, on the angle that I'm cutting to the net and on the speed— all those things. Then I just react."

SAKU KOIVU

Call them garbage goals. That's because rebounds are the easiest way to score. All you do is shovel them into the net. In one survey of 1,200 NHL goals, close to half of them were scored from within 10 feet/3 m of the net. But you must want to score, because right in front of the net can be a painful place to be. Standing in front attracts a lot of attention.

## What to do

1. Form a tripod with your skates and stick.
2. Lean on your stick. Be solid. Think save.
3. Know where the shot is coming from, then watch the goalie's pads. You can't react in time if you watch the shot, but watching the goalie's pads tells you where the rebound will go.
4. Time your arrival at the net. Drive for the net even when the goalie seems to have the puck.

### T I P

High shots are usually caught and held. Low shots create rebounds. So shoot low.

The key to rebounding is to be where the puck will go. Here, a shot from the corner rebounds out front . . .

. . . where Nicolas, now free of his checker, has plenty of room to shoot for the far side.

# Rebounds

## Rebound checklist

- Don't be surprised when a rebound comes your way. Expect it.
- Don't rush your shot. Take your time.
- Use your body to protect the puck. Expect to get hit.
- If a rebound is close to the goalie and the goalie is down, pull it back and shoot high.
- Even when the net is open, shoot hard and try to get the puck off the ice.

Of any close-in play, crossing in front is the one that gives you the most chances to score. In fact, it's better than a breakaway. On a breakaway, you're in a big rush. You're being chased. But if you're crossing in front you take the defense by surprise. Often, you have all the time in the world.

You also have more chances to score when you cross in front. Think about it. On a breakaway you usually get one move, and that move depends on what the goalie is doing. When you cross in front, you make the goalie move sideways across 6 feet/ 1.8 m of goalmouth. That gives you more chances to score. The goalmouth is wide, the puck is small.

So when you find yourself alone with the puck in your opponents' corner, and your teammates are all covered, there is something you can do. Just walk out front—like you own the rink—and take your chances.

# Crossing in front

Michelle holds the near post, so Jordan fakes the shot and goes across. Even when she makes the second save . . .

. . . the rebound gives Jordan a third scoring chance. He buries it.

**TIP**

Any time you can cross in front of the net you give yourself five chances to score—that's better than a breakaway.

## What to do

You have five choices:

1. If the goalie guesses you mean to cross in front, he or she may leave the short-side post as you approach. Watch for this opening. Tuck the puck in the short side.
2. If you are coming from your proper wing, you may be able to break for the front of the net while trailing the puck behind you. When the goalie moves with you, go high to the short side.

3. The goalie cannot move across the net without stepping in the same direction. Fake the shot to hold the goalie at the post. Then, when the goalie opens the pads to go with you, tuck the puck in-between.

4. If the goalie does a double-pad slide across the net, look back. The goalie's upper body will be the last thing to hit the ice. Slide the puck underneath.

5. If none of these openings were there, the goalie is now flat on the ice. Carry the puck past the far post and throw it high.

### Crossing-in-front checklist

■ Watch out for the goalie's poke-check as you get close to the short side. Look for the stick hand to dart up the shaft of the goalie's stick. Be ready to shoot when the goalie lunges at you.

> ### N H L   T I P
> "When you go wide you can gain speed on the outside and then cross in front—it's been a successful move for me."
> **S E R G E I   F E D O R O V**

This time Jordan crosses from his proper (left) wing, fakes the shot to freeze the goalie . . .

. . . and keeps on going, giving himself an open net for a backhand or forehand shot.

# Crossing in front

■ Focus on the net and the goalie. Skate hard. Commit yourself. Aim to cross at the edge of the crease.

■ Look short side first.

■ Next, wait for the goalie's feet to turn and open. Don't shoot the puck between the goalie's legs, just tap or deflect it in when you see the opening.

■ Once you are across—if you haven't already scored yet—look for the backhand over or past the goalie's foot.

Sometimes it comes down to just you and the goalie—one play for all the marbles. When this happens, all you need to do is focus on one thought: *you* have the upper hand. After all, the puck is on your stick. Remember: You decide what's going to happen, so have a plan.

And relax. You know what you're going to do. The goalie doesn't.

## What to do

On a breakaway, there are lots of ways to score. But the move you choose will depend on the goalie's position. Memorize the following breakaway moves, and practise them in your mind and on the ice. Before you make your move, check three things: Is the goalie in or out? Is the goalie playing the angle right? Is the goalie moving sideways?

# Breakaways

Kendall is perfectly positioned—there's not much here to shoot at.

So Will moves right to give himself an angle . . .

. . . and goes to his backhand to make the most of it.

## Is the goalie in or out?

**Goalie in = shot:** If the goalie is back in the net, carry the puck in front to fake the deke, then shoot for the net you can see. Move to your forehand side a bit to improve your angle.

**Goalie out = deke:** If the goalie is out of the net, cutting off the angle, you need to fake the shot, then go around to your forehand side.

**Goalie moves first = shoot for opening:** Some goalies will guess, and make the first move. Go the other way.

## Is the goalie playing the angle right?

Is the goalie playing the angle right, taking away the shot and moving backward to take away the deke? That's what the goalie *should* be doing. Both of you are moving toward the net. The goalie has the advantage.

**Make the goalie move:** Step sideways. Fake one way, then go the other way. No goalie can go two ways at once.

## Is the goalie moving sideways?

Once you have the goalie moving sideways, you have more options. The openings to look for are a lot like the ones you see when you cross in front of the net.

**Goalie moving sideways = between feet:** Watch for the goalie's legs to open. Tap the puck in-between.

Get the goalie moving sideways, and you have an edge.

By going to his backhand, Tyler changes the angle by 4 feet/1.2 m.

The goalie is down and the net is open. Tyler should score.

# Breakaways

## Breakaway checklist

- Prepare for breakaways. Expect them.
- Read and react. Let the goalie tell you what to do.
- Carry the puck in the shooting position.
- If you can—say, on a penalty shot—set up an angle at the blue-line. For example: Turning a bit to your backhand side sets up the off-wing angle at the net. That's the Mario Lemieux way.
- Know which side of the goalie your forehand shot will attack. *Stick side:* shoot low. *Glove side:* shoot high.

"In your own end, it's important to keep your body between the player and the net. If the puck gets behind you, don't let the player get behind you."

ROB BLAKE

# PLAYING BETTER
# DEFENSE

**E**VEN THE BEST players have the puck for less than a minute a game. That leaves 59 minutes when players with average skills can make a difference—if they know how to play defensive hockey.

The basic idea of good defense is this: every player on the ice with the team that doesn't have the puck is a defender. Only a few stars are scoring threats, but *every* player on your team can be useful when your team doesn't have the puck. And if you have good defensive skills, your team will have the puck more. *You* will have it more.

Sometimes you will take the puck away from an opponent. Sometimes it will take teamwork to get the puck. Either way, you will end up having it more. That's a promise.

When you're the defensive player closest to the puck, positioning and angling help you attack the puck carrier.

### Positioning

Positioning refers to where you should be on the ice. In your team's zone, for example, you should be between your check and the goal.

### Angling

Angling is how you approach the puck carrier to get him or her to do what you want. For example: By angling toward the puck carrier from the middle toward the boards on a forecheck, you invite that player to pass the puck up the boards. Your teammate, following you on the forecheck and reading your angle, can figure out where your opponent's pass will go and be there, waiting for the puck to arrive.

# Positioning & angling

The forechecker reads the defender's number. That means attack the puck. Go after it.

The defender has control of the puck. Contain. Play the pass.

### Read and react

This is the time to read and react. If you're the first forechecker, you must read how well the puck carrier is controlling the puck. One key is the crest or number rule. The first forechecker reads the puck carrier: Do you see a sweater crest or number?

- If you see a crest, the puck carrier has control of the puck and has turned toward you. Contain.
- If you see a number, your opponent is trying to gain control of the puck. Attack.

## Sizing up the play

What if you're the second forechecker? The second forechecker also reads and reacts. Don't rush into the play without thinking. You must size up the play deep in the offensive zone. If you're the second forechecker, here's what you look for:

- What angle is the first forechecker taking?
- Where is the first forechecker inviting the puck carrier to move the puck?
- Does the puck carrier have good control?
- Is the first forechecker attacking or containing?
- What kind of support does the puck carrier have? Are there teammates nearby?

These are the first signs that show you how the play will go. The second forechecker reads these signs and goes where the puck is most likely to go—before the puck is released.

The second forechecker goes where the pass was sent, takes control of the puck and looks for a third teammate in front of the net.

Meanwhile, the passer is eliminated by forechecker number one.

# Positioning & angling

## Putting it together

This is where teamwork comes in. The second forechecker must read what his or her teammate is inviting the puck carrier to do, and react by going where the puck is likely to go. If the first forechecker can take the puck or if that second player can intercept the pass, the two forecheckers, working together, will have a good chance to score.

Defense to offense—in a split second!

You are now close to the puck carrier on the forecheck, or the puck carrier is coming at you in your own zone. This is the moment to take the puck.

### Poke-check

This is the best move to use when the puck carrier is approaching you head-on. Hold your stick with your top hand only and thrust directly at the puck, with your stickblade flat on the ice. Don't lose your balance.

### Sweep-check

This check works best from in front or slightly to one side against a good stickhandler. Instead of poking directly at the puck, sweep your stick low to the ice so it hits the puck carrier's stick.

# Stick-checks

Poke-check. Go right at the puck, top hand on the stick, head up.

Sweep-check: Covers more ice, and forces the puck carrier to get rid of the puck.

### TIP

Be very careful not to lift your opponent's stick above waist level. This is how many stick-related injuries occur.

### Stick lift

Use a stick lift when approaching an opposing puck carrier from behind or at an angle. Move your lower hand down your stick for leverage. Lift your opponent's stick from low on the shaft, then skate through the puck and pick it up with your back skateblade.

### Stick press

The opposite of lifting your opponent's stick. Just use your stick to press your opponent's stick down. Aim for the blade-to-handle joint.

Body checking may not be allowed at your playing level. But body contact *will* take place when 10 kids, all of them after one puck, are skating in a confined area. The ability to make legal contact is an important skill in hockey. It is also a good way to prepare yourself for full-contact hockey in a few years' time.

## Blocking the way

It is legal for a defender to block the way of the puck carrier— as long as the defender is in the lane first. You can not step into the puck carrier's path.

In your own zone, getting between your check and the net is your first task. If your check gets the puck and you are in position, you will be blocking the way. This is hard to do. But being in the puck carrier's way makes you a good defensive player.

**T I P**

It is important to learn how to control offensive players without hitting them, no matter what level of hockey you are playing. Good defensive skills are often the key to moving up to the next level.

The checker can simply skate the puck carrier off the puck and take control.

Leaning into the puck carrier along the boards is legal . . .

. . . and so is simply stepping between the puck carrier and the puck.

**Body contact**

## Leaning into the puck carrier

If you and the puck carrier are going in the same direction, you can lean into him or her. You may even be able to deflect the puck carrier from his or her path. Keep your feet moving to stay with the puck carrier. To prevent a penalty, do not hook or hold your opponent.

When body checking is not allowed, you can not finish a check by running the puck carrier into the boards. In fact, you can't check anyone but the puck carrier.

**ONCE YOU KNOW** how to read and react and angle in on the puck carrier, you perform these skills without thinking. The next step is to combine your skating and checking skills, so that you are using them together and at the right times.

This is where you really learn the game of hockey from the inside out. When NHL players talk about winning by doing the little things right, they're talking about being in position and knowing who to check.

There are certain plays that happen again and again during games. You can learn to read those plays and react the right way—every time.

Make playing solid defense a habit. It can be just as much fun as scoring goals, and you can do it more often.

# the inside game

DEFENSE

"I like to keep my speed and not lose it, and maybe circle behind the net and build up speed from there."

SCOTT NIEDERMAYER

We are calling these actions skills, because they require practise to learn. But you will want to make them habits.

### Head on a swivel

First, you have to see what's happening to be able to read the play. Be aware at all times of where everyone is. You probably do this when you are skating toward a loose puck, so you'll know what to do when you get there. But make it a habit all the time.

### Quick feet

Second, you have to be in position to make the check. To do that, always maintain your momentum. Keep your feet moving, never coast. When you lose the puck, stop, turn the other way and go get it back.

# Reading the play

The puck carrier comes from behind the net at full speed, with good puck control. Don't commit. Contain.

The puck carrier is coming at you hard. Maintain the gap. Back off.

### Read and react

There is no one play that shows all the ways to read and react on the ice. Reading and reacting to what's going on around you is more than a skill you'll use in just a few situations. It's a way of being more aware of the game and your part in it—all the time.

Reading and reacting is a better way to play hockey. It's a skill that will make you a better player anywhere on the ice. An example of a read-and-react skill is reading the gap between you and the puck carrier.

The gap is the amount of space between you and the play. Controlling the size of the gap between you and the puck gives you an edge: You can invite the puck carrier to do what you want by deciding whether to attack the puck or hold off and contain. Remember: The key question is, should I attack or contain?

## Read the gap

The smaller the gap between you and the puck carrier, the higher the risk of the puck carrier going around you—and the better your chance of making the check. The closer you are to the puck the more you're at risk, and the more you're committed to making the check. Whether you move in to attack or back off and contain depends on how well the puck carrier is controlling the puck, and on how much support you have from your teammates.

---

**T I P**

Controlling the gap is one way to put pressure on the puck carrier—or to take pressure off.

---

As Nicolas slows up, he closes the gap, inviting Danny to go outside.

When Danny reads the wide gap, he could choose to cut across in front of Nicolas. Nicolas must move sideways to defend.

*Gap control*

The bigger the gap, the more time and space the puck carrier has to make a play. You must be ready to go in any direction.

Remember: By controlling the size of the gap between you and the puck, you invite the puck carrier to do what you want.

## Read the gap checklist

- **Close the gap:** You force the puck carrier to beat you one-on-one or to get rid of the puck quickly.
- **Open the gap:** You invite the puck carrier to try to make a play.

You know *what* gap control is, but how do you know *when* to attack and when to contain? Answer: It depends on how well the puck carrier is controlling the puck.

■ If your opponent has poor puck control, go hard for the puck.

■ If your opponent has good puck control, back off and contain.

What if you're skating toward an opponent who is going for a loose puck?

■ If you can see the player's number, attack the puck.

■ If you can see the player's sweater crest, contain.

Why? If you can see the player's number, your opponent has his or her back to you and is still picking up the puck. Attack. (Don't bump your opponent into the boards. Approach at an angle.)
But if you can see the player's crest, that means your opponent has control, has turned around with the puck and is looking to make a play. Contain.

# *Attack or contain?*

The opponent turns toward the boards to pick up the puck.
Attack, but be careful of the boards.

Your opponent has control. You see the crest. Contain.

**TIP**
Gap control is a tool you can use anywhere on the ice—except near your own net.

## Attack or contain checklist

■ Is the puck carrier coming at you hard? Back off, contain, and keep yourself in the play.

■ Are you outnumbered? Contain and try to prevent the pass. Stall for time until help arrives from your teammates.

■ Is the puck carrier having problems handling the puck? Attack.

## What is the mid-ice lane?

The mid-ice lane runs up and down the ice surface from goal-mouth to goalmouth and between the faceoff dots. The team that has the puck has to move it into the lane in front of its opponents' goal to have the best chance of scoring. The defensive team tries to keep the puck out of that lane—out along the boards.

When you think about it, this only makes sense. On a power play, the penalty killers allow the puck to move around the outside of their defensive zone. They also work hard to keep it out of the slot, or shooting zone.

So hockey is played within three marked zones—and inside and outside an unmarked zone. The marked zones are contained by the bluelines, which run from side to side. The unmarked zone—the mid-ice lane—runs the length of the ice, from goal line to goal line.

### NHL TIP

"When I work harder at those one-on-one battles I get the puck more often. I don't wait for the puck, I go after it. My defense creates my offense."

**MIKE MODANO**

Always keep the mid-ice lane in mind when defending. Inside the lane, at either end, attack the puck. Outside the lane, contain.

The defender is playing on the shooter's inside shoulder, inviting him or her to go outside.

# *The mid-ice lane*

## Controlling the mid-ice lane

You must be aware of this unmarked zone to play defensive hockey well. Most of the dangerous scoring chances in a game are created here. The more you can keep the attacking team out of the mid-ice lane, the fewer goals you are likely to give up.

This is the battle that goes on as long as the game lasts. Every time you decide whether to attack the puck or contain the puck carrier, your decision will depend partly on where the puck is within this invisible zone that runs the length of the ice.

Remember, when the other team has the puck:

- control play in the mid-ice lane, and
- force your opponents to shoot from outside.

### Playing the mid-ice lane

Think about this end-to-end zone when your opponents have the puck—no matter where you are on the ice. Attack the puck if the puck carrier is in front of your net—or your opponents' net.

Always attack the puck if it's near the net—either net. Both of these areas are within the mid-ice lane.

If your opponent has good control of the puck, you might want to try and keep him or her along the boards. Your opponent is not dangerous there. Try to block a pass into the middle, where your opponents are more of a threat.

# The mid-ice lane

Front of the net: watch the puck, stay in touch with your check.

Head on a swivel: stickblade on the ice, eyes on the receiver. That's your check.

### Mid-ice checklist

- Give your opponents the outside—deny them the middle.
- Attack the puck at either net.
- Block passes into the middle.
- Stay on the inside of your check.
- When the other team has the puck, protect the mid-ice lane. Keep your opponents out of this lane, and they're less likely to score.

# the defensive zone

**IN HOCKEY**, you make decisions about what to do several times in a single shift. What you do depends on where you are on the ice.

Your defensive zone is the Danger Zone. This is where you must stay alert, read the play and react the fastest. Making a check near your own goal can be as satisfying as scoring a goal—it is just as important.

The rules are simple. Stay between your check and the net. Look for the puck. Keep your stick on the ice. Protect the middle.

One good thing about defending in your own zone is that you know where your opponents are trying to put the puck. Wait long enough, be in the right place and the puck will come to you.

### Positioning

The first rule of defending in your own zone is to pick up your check and stay between that player and the net.

Most of the time, just being with your check will eliminate him or her from the play. But don't just shadow your check. Look around. Keep in touch. Use your stick to feel where your check is as you look away for the puck.

Leave your check only when you see your chance to take the puck. Be 100 per cent sure. If there is any doubt, stay in position rather than going for the puck.

### Pressure or contain?

In your own zone, more than anywhere else on the ice, you want to go after the puck when your check has it. If you take the puck your team's problem is solved. Miss, and things go from bad to worse.

# The danger zone

Pass from the corner: eyes on the puck, stick on your opponent's stick.

The puck carrier skates out of the corner. Stay with your check, let the goalie take the shooter.

So it has to be controlled pressure. That means there are times when you should contain instead of pressuring.

For example, when the puck carrier is coming out of the corner and has a teammate in the slot, the puck carrier has two options: go to the net, or pass. You must contain. Do your job, and stay with your check. This forces the puck carrier to go to the net. Let your goalie take the shooter.

## When to contain

- When you're the last line of defense.
- When missing the check would give your opponent a scoring chance. Let the puck carrier come to you. A good example is when the puck carrier comes out of the corner. Missing the check would put the puck carrier alone in front of the net. So back off. Stay between him or her and the net.
- When you're outnumbered near your own net. Again, don't take yourself out of the play by going for the puck. Let the goalie take the puck carrier. Stay between your opponents and play the pass.

## When to attack

Sooner or later, the play will come close to your net and you will have to pressure the puck carrier. Force the puck carrier to make a good pass or take a shot on goal.

### T I P
Don't panic. Just because your opponents have the puck in your zone doesn't mean they'll score. Stay cool. Cover your check and wait for the puck to come your way.

Covering the point: face your check, eyes on the puck.

The player covering in front only goes for the puck when 100 per cent sure of taking possession.

# The danger zone

- Don't leave your feet—that will take you out of the play. Don't try to deflect an incoming shot. Let your goalie see the puck.
- If your team is running around, try to get a whistle. Freeze the puck against the boards. Fall on it if you can. Ice the puck, or at least get it out of the zone.
- If your opponents score, don't blame anyone else. Don't bang your stick on the ice. Stay cool.

## Controlling your opponent

Any player on your team might have to cover the front of your net. This is where you can make the difference between the other team scoring or your team taking the puck in the other direction. This is where the puck will arrive, sooner or later.

Just being with your check in the slot is not enough. You have to know where the puck is and control your opponent in different ways, depending on where the shot may come from. Your head is on a swivel. You look from the puck to your check, and back again.

## Read and react

**If the puck is in the corner:** Stay between your check and the puck. That means watching for the pass but staying in touch with your check. Leave your check only when you are 100 per cent sure the puck is yours.

# In front of the net

The defender has good net-side coverage of the most dangerous player—the one in front of the net. Goalie takes the shooter.

**T I P**

In front of the net, think rebound. Anticipate where the rebound will go and be there first.

**If the puck is at the point:** You need to do two things. First, stay in contact with your check. Know the path your check wants to take and block that path. If your opponent is screening the goalie's view, move him or her out of the way.

Second, when the shot comes, control your check's stick. Lift it to prevent a deflection and to keep your check from scoring on a rebound.

DEFENSE
# *the neutral zone*

**HOW THINGS GO** in your own zone depends on how they went in the neutral zone. Problems in the neutral zone become scoring chances at your net.

The neutral zone is where a smart defender can really shine. By hustling back to help you can even up the odds when your team is outnumbered at your blueline. Skate hard coming back; your coach will be sure to notice. Just by being with your check, you allow your defense to play on the blueline rather than backing in.

When the defense is able to stand up and play on the blueline, two good things can happen for your team. A cross-ice pass will end up on a defender's stick or an opponent will be forced to go off-side. Either way, the rush is over.

The other team has the puck and they're coming at you. What do you do? Look to see who has the edge. Is your team outnumbered? Do you have a numbers advantage, or are the numbers even?

### How to do it

**If the numbers are even:** If it's one-on-one, two-on-two or three-on-three, take the player nearest you. Stay with your check. If your check is the puck carrier, make sure he or she loses control of the puck. Always protect the middle. Remember: On even-numbered plays, you still have the advantage. Win each of the one-on-ones and you win the five-on-five.

**If the defense outnumbers the attackers:** Immediately pressure the puck carrier. If the puck carrier is your check or the player closest to you, take him or her. Block his or her way to the net. Don't worry about the puck.

# Playing the rush

Two-on-two: The defender nearest to the puck can attack the shooter, because his teammate has eliminated the other forward.

### TIP
Watch for two attackers to criss-cross to disrupt your coverage. When that happens, stay with your check.

**If you're outnumbered:** If the play is two-on-one, three-on-one or three-on-two, try to stall the attack until help comes. Allow moves to the outside, deny passes into the middle. Let the goaltender take the puck carrier. Remember, the key points are:

- Stall. Take the inside position between the play and your net. Contain your opponent.
- Defend the middle. Deny passes into the slot. Let the goaltender take the shot.

Even when you don't have the puck, there is one aspect of the attack you can control: the gap between you and the play. By playing tight to the play or loose, a few steps away, you are telling the puck carrier what to do.

## How to do it

**When you play tight:** This means you invite the puck carrier to beat you. Play tight when the numbers are even or better, and when you feel confident the puck carrier can't beat you.

**When you play loose:** Leave a larger gap, and you invite the puck carrier to turn sideways or make a play. Keep a wide gap when you're outnumbered, or when the puck carrier has good control.

Remember: Playing the gap in the neutral zone is like deciding whether to attack or contain the puck carrier, except that you read and react to a play that involves several players.

Nicolas plays the puck carrier tight, forcing his opponent to pass or go around him.

Outnumbered? Keep a loose gap. Brian wants to prevent a pass to Kellin in the middle.

# Playing the gap

## Heads up

Watch for the rink-wide pass. On the rush, the most dangerous players are the ones away from the puck.

When your team is guarding its blueline well and trying to check the opposition outside your defensive zone, the puck carrier has two choices: a rink-wide pass or a shot into your zone. Both can result in your team getting the puck back. A rink-wide pass at your blueline can be a turnover if you're expecting it.

## Defense to offense

Intercepting a rink-wide pass outside your own blueline is one of the many ways you can start a lightning-quick turnaround in the neutral zone.

The whole idea of playing good defense is to get the puck and move it in the other direction. If you can do it when your opponents are skating hard into your zone, that's even better. You can catch them going the wrong way.

As soon as you have the puck at your own blueline, look up-ice for a teammate coming back late. Put the puck on his or her stick and the result may be a breakaway.

So don't wait. Look for the quick pass first or carry the puck yourself. Get going in the other direction!

# Transition

The blue team has lost the puck. Danny, in red, reads the play and looks for a pass . . .

Scott slams on the brakes, eyeballs the play and starts in the other direction. He is already in a position to intercept a pass to Danny.

## Stay with your check

If your team loses the puck in the neutral zone you become an instant defender. Don't coast in a big circle. Stop, then find your check. Place yourself between your check and the puck.

If your check has the puck, you're probably nearby and in a position to make the check. So stop dead, turn around and go for the puck. In the neutral zone, you are likely to be skating in the same direction as your check. This is the ideal position for making stick-checks.

## Reading and reacting

Almost everything you do while defending in the neutral zone involves reading and reacting. The difference in the neutral zone is that you're reading the big picture.

## What to look for

- Are you outnumbered? If so, is help from your team on the way?
- Are they coming hard, with good puck control? Offer them a wide gap and stay in the play.
- Protect the middle. Allow your opponents to go wide but deny the pass into the mid-ice lane.
- Look for the rink-wide pass at the blueline. It's your chance to turn defense into offense in a split second.

### N H L  T I P

"Players sometimes forget that preventing goals is as important as scoring. I take a defense-first attitude in my approach to the game—every night."

M I C H A E L   P E C A

The tables are turned: The blue team gets the puck. Scott looks for the pass and Danny must react.

Danny has two strides to make up. He wants to get to Scott's inside shoulder to prevent a pass to Scott.

*Transition*

## Be a quick-change artist

Good defensive players often score key goals in tight games. The key to making the most of a turnover is to strike fast—to catch your opponents skating the wrong way.

- If you have the puck, turn and look to make the quick pass.
- If you see the turnover happen, make yourself available for a pass. One way to do that is to skate hard across the ice, so your teammate with the puck can spot you.
- Learn to take passes from directly behind you.

**PLAYING WELL DEFENSIVELY** has many rewards, but none feel as good as taking the puck from your opponents in their own zone—and then scoring.

You have that chance when you forecheck hard in the offensive zone. Here, more than anywhere else on the ice, is where you cash in the fastest. So be aggressive. Go in hard. Make your opponents move the puck faster than they would like to. Sometimes, when they are rushed, they will put the puck on one of your teammate's sticks.

Your chances of scoring are better than on the rush because you'll be taking your opponents by surprise. One moment they have the puck and are starting the breakout. The next moment they are fishing it out of their own net.

# *the offensive zone*

## DEFENSE

## Steering the play

As you know, the first forechecker into the offensive zone attacks the puck by approaching the puck carrier *at an angle*, denying the pass where the forechecker is coming from and inviting a pass in the other direction.

Sometimes the puck carrier will try to pass through the forechecker. That's the forechecker's chance to take the puck. More often, the puck carrier will take the invitation to pass.

## Pressure on the puck

Most of the time, it takes two players to steal the puck on the forecheck. The first forechecker steers the play. He or she approaches the puck carrier at an angle, such as coming from the slot toward the corner, to force the puck up the boards.

Forechecking takes teamwork. The first forechecker steers the play.

If you are the first forechecker, go hard for the puck. Make the puck carrier get rid of it.

**Force the play**

You want the puck carrier and your teammates to see where you are inviting your opponent to pass the puck. The second forechecker reads the direction open to the puck carrier to pass or go to, and goes there.

If the second forechecker sees his teammate angle in on the puck carrier from the middle, he knows the first forechecker is inviting the puck carrier to move the puck up the boards. Reading these cues tells the second forechecker to go to the boards.

The puck comes up the boards, and bingo!—scoring chance.

### Creating the turnover

Picking up a loose puck along the boards is one way to create turnovers in the offensive zone. But there are actually more ways to take control of the puck in your opponents' zone than anywhere else on the ice.

In the offensive zone, every forward should attack the puck hard. If you miss there will be a second chance. Always make sure your angle of attack takes away one option and invites another. If you have a choice, try to take away the mid-ice lane. Make your opponents move the puck along the boards. It is easier to keep the puck in your opponents' zone along the boards.

By forechecking hard, you press your opponents to make decisions faster than they want to. Often they will cough up the puck.

# Get the puck

The second forechecker reads the teammate's angle of attack and anticipates where the puck will go . . .

. . . and goes to that spot, looking for a third teammate to pass to.

Each time a forechecker attacks the puck, he or she creates the chance for a turnover. Either the forechecker takes the puck or the teammate who is giving support goes where the puck is likely to go. Anticipate!

Finally, just playing most of the game in your opponents' zone can create turnovers. Players under pressure to make a quick play often hand the puck over to their opponents.

## Eliminate your check

The moment your team loses control of the puck in the offensive zone, don't be lazy. Look for your check and pick him or her up. Stay between your check and the puck to make sure they're not open for a pass. Just by being there, you keep your check from being part of your opponents' breakout. It's almost like making them play shorthanded.

If your check has the puck, be aggressive. Try to take the puck away before your check gets out of the zone. If you get control, shoot the puck deep into the zone.

## Reading and reacting

Forechecking in the offensive zone is reading and reacting in its purest form.

**T I P**
Stay alert for the pass up the middle. Stealing the puck in the mid-ice lane of your opponents' zone is a defender's dream come true.

Kellin looks for a pass as Nicolas reacts to his team losing the puck...

...but Nicolas catches up as Kellin gains control, preventing a pass into the middle.

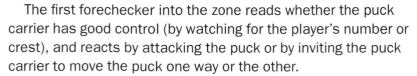

*Keep control*

The first forechecker into the zone reads whether the puck carrier has good control (by watching for the player's number or crest), and reacts by attacking the puck or by inviting the puck carrier to move the puck one way or the other.

The second player into the zone reads where the first forechecker is inviting the puck carrier to move the puck, and goes there.

Remember: Read the play to see where the puck will go, then react by going there in time to make a play.

# SHUTOUT

## GOALTENDING

**A**s **A GOALTENDER**, how well you play depends on how well you prepare. There is no time to get ready once the puck drops. NHL goaltenders will tell you that the mental aspects of playing this demanding position are more important than how you move in the net. Many great athletes don't make it as goalies at the top level; watching them play, you wonder how some star goaltenders do it.

Work out a routine that begins at least a couple of hours before the game—one that gets you relaxed and in the right frame of mind before you step on the ice for your warmup. And remember, your warmup doesn't get you ready to play. It's the finishing touch to your pre-game routine.

### Concentrate

Depending on how you rate your opponents, you might start worrying about an upcoming game days ahead. It's healthy to be concerned about how you will play. It means you care. But worrying doesn't help. Channel all that energy and get it working for you. Use it to focus and concentrate on the game—starting a few hours before the referee drops the puck.

### Visualize

A few hours before you step on the ice, begin visualizing yourself making saves. Start getting ready for the impact of the puck by *feeling* it hit you. You have the angle right, so the puck always hits you. Next, start extending the movements you are imagining. Feel yourself turning low shots into the corners with your stick and feet, or flexing your knees as you rise to take high shots off your chest. Finally, use your imagination to put yourself in the game, anticipating plays.

# *Pre-game routine*

Imagine yourself making big saves: high shots, low shots, dekes, breakaways.

Be at the rink early. Check your equipment. Give yourself time to put it on right.

### Be prepared

You wear more equipment than any other team-game player, so give yourself lots of time to put it on right. Rushing when you're dressing means loose buckles and straps under your skate-blades, and you know when you will discover them. You will be first on the ice, so be the first dressed—always.

## Warmup

Work hard in the warmup. This is the place and time to work into a rhythm: find a groove and be ready for a two-on-one or a breakaway off the opening faceoff. Expect either. Some goalies use the rock music at the warmup to get their bodies moving to a beat. Finding the right tempo can carry you through the game.

## Warmup guidelines

- Your teammates need to take it easy with their first shots. Have them hit you in the pads, *before* they shoot at the lower corners.
- There is no excuse for your teammates to shoot high in the warmup. The warmup is for you, the goalie, not for your team's shooters to practise roofing the puck. Remember, players who shoot high often believe they are warming up your hands. But your hands don't need warming up—your feet do.

> **N H L   T I P**
> "Part of my warmup routine includes an intensive stretch—it allows me to be nice and loose to prevent any muscle pulls."
> **G R A N T   F U H R**

Easy shots at first. Work on doing it right in the warmup. Watch the puck into your glove.

Start making the puck your focus. React to it, let it guide you, and then start controlling rebounds. Be in command.

## The warmup

No goalie steps onto the ice ready to make saves with his or her feet, and that's where most shots come.

- Don't allow your teammates to skate in and shoot when others are shooting from the blueline. Limit the number of pucks.
- Never allow your teammates to deke you when you're cold—unless they want a goalie with a strained groin muscle.

**YOU CAN'T** be thinking about each move during a game. Everything you do has to be instinctive. You see the puck, you stop it. It's as simple as that.

For your movements in the net to become habits, you have to practise until they become second nature. Some goalies don't like practising—why collect bruises with no points on the line? Here's why: There's no time to think with the puck on your doorstep and a game to be won. There's an old saying in sports, that luck comes from preparation. Great saves often *look* lucky, but how you practise is how you play.

Once the game begins, stop thinking and react. Focus. Make stopping the puck your only task in life.

# *into the game*

### GOALTENDING

## The ready position

As a goaltender, all your moves start with you standing still. If your stance, or ready position, is not right, making the proper moves will be difficult, or impossible. For example, if your ready position doesn't allow you to keep your stickblade on the ice, you will give up bad goals no matter what else you do.

## What to do

No matter which style you play, you have to be in the ready position and in the right place *before* the puck arrives. Doing the splits or reaching with your catcher look good, but either move means you were out of position.

You want to be as big in the net as you can be. That means being square to the puck, on the shot line, with your stickblade

**T I P**
Most goals are scored against goalies who are out of their stance.

Many goalies bend too much at the waist. Bend at the knees and keep your upper body up, so the puck can hit it.

Your stance should be relaxed. Flex your knees to keep your stickblade on the ice.

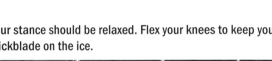

*Stance*

flat on the ice. Most problems in goaltending come from failures in one or more of these three areas.

Your biggest pieces of equipment are your leg pads and upper-body protector. Your ready position must make the most of these big pads. So think about how you sit in a chair: your lower legs and chest are almost vertical. Then think of yourself as sitting in the ready position—without the chair, of course—with your lower legs and chest available for the puck to hit. That's the way to cover the most net. You'll feel the strain in the big muscles of your thighs.

### Stance checklist

The rest of the ready position depends on your style. Try some of these ideas:

- Improve your side-to-side balance by keeping your hands level with each other.
- Remember, every shot comes from ice level. The closer the shooter, the more likely the shot will come in low. Also, it's easier to lift your catching glove than lower it.
- Keep both gloves in front of your body. That will help you see every shot right into your glove and keep the puck in front of you. Another advantage of keeping your hands out front is that, as you are seen by the shooter, the gaps between your body and your arms will close. This makes you look more solid.
- One sign of a good goalie is when you see very little movement.

# Stance

Holding your gloves level helps keep you balanced.

When your gloves are ahead of your body, the gaps between your arms and body close, and it's easier to see the puck into your gloves.

**T I P**

In the ready position, don't bend over from the waist. Flex your knees, not your hips. Keep your back as straight as possible.

The puck hits good goalies just as it finds the sticks of good scorers. It's all a matter of angles.

- Felix Potvin knows that even butterfly goalies need to play their angles. You may be covering more of the ice surface, but you can't move much once you are down.
- Know how the elbow on your stick side feels with your stick-blade flat on the ice—in both positions, on your feet and in the butterfly. Patrick Roy made sure he had his hands up when he was on his knees.

# GOALTENDING
## *footwork*

**BY BEING IN LINE** with the shooter, a goalie covers as much of the net as possible. Being on the line a shot must travel to enter the centre of the net is called "playing the angle."

Position is everything when you're a goalie. You must know where the puck will go before it is shot and be waiting in the ready position. In other words, you must anticipate the play. There are two aspects to playing angles: side-to-side movements and gliding in and out of the net. The key is to move ahead, back or sideways without losing your ready position.

Nothing about goaltending is easy, but moving around while keeping square to the shooter and in your stance is the biggest step you can take toward being a reliable goalie.

Goaltenders are the most important players on the ice. Nowhere else is reading and reacting and moving quickly more important than in the net. For a goalie, footwork, edge control and agility are vital. As a goaltender, you can play your position using a mix of styles. But, whatever style works for you, there are some skills all goalies must master.

## Positioning

You can't stop the puck if you are not in position. Positioning is made up of three parts:

- Your angle, which means being on the line from the puck to the middle of the net.
- Your depth in the net along that line.
- Your balanced stance.

# Goalie footwork

Tory is standing up on the shot line. He can reach any shot that is on the net.

A C-cut with the inside front edge of his right skate starts him back into the net.

After backing in to the post, Tory starts across the goalmouth with a T-push.

Each is important, but none more than angle. Even if you've got a great glove hand, it's no good to you if you can't reach the puck.

Once you are on that shot line, move in or out, depending on where the shooter is. For point shots, be at the edge of the crease. As the shooter comes closer, be ready to back in to cover the deke.

Even butterfly goalies spend most of the time on their feet. Stand on your inside front edges and balance your stance: front to back with a deep knee bend so your stickblade is flat on the ice, and side to side with your feet wider than your shoulders.

"Movement and footwork are the keys to positioning. Practise moving post to post, out along the shot line and back into the net every time you step on the ice."

ROBERTO LUONGO

When the puck is far away from the net, move out. As the puck moves to one side, back up toward the net and to that side. Or, if a lone shooter comes in on the wing, move out to challenge the shooter. If no shot comes, start moving back into the net as the shooter passes the circle hash marks—in case the shooter tries to go around you. Think of yourself as being attached to your posts by big elastic bands. Move with the play. The puck controls you.

## How to do it

A goalie glides in and out with small movements of the ankles and feet. That is why goaltenders have to be good skaters. They must move around the ice as quickly as other players, but without using their bodies for leverage. All the power is generated from the knees down.

# In & out

Kendall's solid stance and correct angle on the puck allows her to cover a lot of the net from inside the crease...

...but she covers almost all of it by coming out on a line with the puck. Go for the top corner? She dares you.

**TIP**

*Come out* to play the shot, then *back in* to play the deke.

Ian Young, a respected goaltending coach, calls the in-and-out movement "telescoping." As you move toward the shooter, you get bigger and block more of the net.

As with every rule in goaltending, there is an exception. If an opposition player appears to either side of you, you must cheat back to the net and a bit toward that side. Sometimes goalies have to do two things at once. You still focus on the shooter, as always. Don't be distracted. Stay on the line of the shot. Stopping the shot is still your main job. But be ready to react to the pass.

**100**

And what if the puck is moving from side to side?

You have to move with it. There are four ways to get across the goalmouth: two "up" moves and two "down" moves. The most common up moves are the T-push and the shuffle. Use an up move when the play is still outside the faceoff dots. The closer the shooter or the pass across the crease, the faster you must get across. That's the time for a down move.

## The T-push

The easiest way to cross the goal is with a T-push. Point outward with the toe of the foot on the side you want to move to. Push off the front inside edge of the other skate. Shift your weight to the glide skate. Keep your knees flexed. That helps you hold your normal stance, gives you better extension and helps keep your

Tory T-pushes to his stick side. Lead leg turned out, pointed where he's going.

The shuffle. Tory takes big steps, but keeps his stance while moving sideways.

He keeps his stick on the ice all the time. One more step takes him to the post.

**Up moves**

stick on the ice. Plus, it makes it easier to stop exactly where you want to. Learn to go from post to post with one push.

## The shuffle

With the puck closer, shuffle across. The shuffle keeps you in your shot-blocking stance all the way across. Keeping your toes pointing straight ahead, take a small step sideways with the foot on the side you want to move to. Then close your legs by bringing the back foot under you. Repeat as many times as you have to. Keep your knees flexed. Stay square to the puck.

When the puck crosses near the crease, you need to slide from post to post quickly. There are two ways to do it in one move—stacking the pads and the butterfly slide. When you get there, most of the goalmouth is covered down low.

## Stacking the pads

Stacking the pads is one way to defend against a pass from one side of the net to a receiver on the open side. You want that receiver to see a wall of goal pads. This is a big-save move.

### How to do it

Start with a T-push in the direction you want to move, pushing off hard with the inside front edge of your back skate. Flex both knees, so your back leg pad is down on the ice as your upper body leans back. Bend your lead leg, then extend it across the

# Down moves

Tory begins with a T-push, fully extending his trailing leg.

Knees flexed, the trailing pad is now sweeping under his body.

He stacks his pads, adds his glove for height and keeps his stick ready for a return pass.

goalmouth. When your trailing knee and hip hit the ice, sweep that back leg along the ice to a position under the lead pad.

As you finish, your pads should be staggered. Keep the top pad ahead of the bottom one to block a quick-rising shot or deflection.

Complete the move by placing your upper arm along the top pad to make the stack a little higher. If it's your glove hand, you are ready to catch a shot or deflection going higher than your stack. If it's your blocker hand, you've got another 75 square inches/480 sq. cm of the wide part of your stick to work with. Reach out your low arm square to your body along the ice to control a return pass or rebound.

## Butterfly slide

Not all young goalies can do the butterfly slide. It takes strength and flexibility. And, the bigger you are, the more effective this move is. But, if you can do it, the butterfly slide is a way to get across the goalmouth in one move. You can keep your eyes on the puck more easily than when you stack the pads.

## How to do it

As with the T-push, your back foot points ahead of your body. Reach with the leg on the side you want to move to, and push off

**T I P**
Keep your chest high doing the butterfly slide. You are going down, opening up the upper part of the net. Keeping your chest up helps cover that opening up high.

Push off hard from the post, keeping the lead pad square to the shooter.

Tory's pads are almost flat on the ice, covering everything but the five-hole . . .

. . . which he shuts with his trailing pad. He keeps compact. His body is upright.

# Down moves

hard with the inside front edge of your back foot. Get your lead pad down fast and slide to the opposite post. Now bring the trailing pad quickly to the ice and close the five-hole with it.

The trick is to keep yourself compact. Keep your arms tightly at your sides, and close that five-hole fast when you get to the other side. Finish with your stick covering what's left of the five-hole. Or set it paddle-down to cover more of the ice.

"I'm able to play as many minutes as I do because I take care of myself. The key is to have strong legs and a strong core— to limit the groin and stomach injuries that a goalie usually faces."

OLAF KOLZIG

GOALTENDING

# *read and react*

**STAYING IN THE GAME** means knowing the game situation and watching what's going on around you. You see more of the ice than anyone on your team, so help your teammates out: tell them when they're in trouble, or when they have lots of time to make the play.

Grant Fuhr once said that it takes two mistakes to allow a goal. One of those two mistakes is made by the netminder. Shoulder your part of the responsibility.

You are the only one who is on the ice all the time. So be a leader. Set an example. Give credit when things go right, take responsibility when things go wrong.

One more thing. Be cool.

### The odd-even rule

When your opponents cross the blueline in front of you, check first to see if your defense is outnumbered.

If it's three-on-three, or any other equal number, come well out to the top of the crease and face the shooter. With the teams at even strength in your zone, a pass is less likely.

If your team is outnumbered and the opposition has an odd man, think pass. Come out only to the edge of the crease.

### Stepping into the line of fire

Stay alert by moving with the puck, even when it is deep in the other end of the ice. Move sideways and in and out; imagine that you and the puck are connected. Relax, but keep your eyes on the puck. Some goalies concentrate on the puck even during stoppages in play.

# Into your zone

Here the defender is outnumbered. Take the shooter but be ready for a pass. Don't come out too far.

Make sure it's a shootaround before you leave the net.

Move out past the crease and into your crouch or ready position when your opponents bring the puck across the centre redline. But don't root yourself to the spot. Not just yet.

Look for the puck carrier to shoot the puck around your endboards as soon as the centre line is crossed. Only by anticipating the shootaround can you get behind the net fast enough to stop it for your defense.

## Handling shootarounds

Your opponents can be out of your zone as fast as they came in if you handle dump-ins right.

Try to field the puck by skating behind the net on the side the puck is shot from. Return by the same side. This helps your defense avoid running into you.

As you turn to go behind your net, watch the puck as it skips around the corner toward you. If the ice is rough at the base of the corner boards, the puck can be deflected in front of your net. Be careful.

Look both ways as you move behind the net. If an opponent is likely to arrive, move the puck yourself. Get it as high on the glass as you can.

When you field the puck from your stick side, face the backboards and stop the puck with the back side of your stick.

### TIP

When you're not in the net at practice, carry a puck with you. Work on the same stickhandling and shooting skills your teammates are practising.

Low right side, right-handed goalie: trap the puck with your stick.

High on the boards: get your body on the wall to control the puck.

Left side: easy for a right-handed goalie. Leave the puck away from the boards.

# Shootarounds

You can seal off the backboards better from your glove side—on that side you can set your body against the wall and set the toe of your stick against the ice-level dasher. Leave the puck 12 inches/30 cm or so from the dasher.

A word of warning: Make sure it's a shootaround before you leave your net. Don't cheat by leaving early. Better to miss the dump-in than have a shooter in front and you out of the net.

### Two-on-one

Call it out to the defense: "*Two*-on-one."

Two things can happen. The puck carrier can shoot or pass. You cover the shot. Your defense is watching for the pass. If the shooter shows signs of wanting to pass, fine. But you are committed to the shooter as long as that player has the puck and is moving toward the net. Don't anticipate, but be aware of the open player.

As soon as the puck carrier passes, react. What you do depends on how close the pass receiver is.

**Far out:** If the pass is far out of your reach, T-push across, staying on your feet.

**In close:** If the puck is in close, you may be able to deflect the pass. If not, stack your pads: slide feet-first to the far post.

# *On the rush*

On a two-on-one rush, the goalie plays the shooter. Leave the pass to the defender...

...until the other attacker has the puck. Try to come across on your feet—if possible.

If the pass is in close, try to kick out with your lower leg pad before that player can redirect the puck. Don't think about it. Stacking your pads is an instinctive, split-second reaction.

### Three-on-one

Make sure it *is* a three-on-one. Is somebody getting back to cancel part of the advantage? If not, call it out. Play deep in your net. Play the shooter, but not as aggressively. Respond to a pass as you would to a two-on-one, but try to stay on your feet.

## Breakaways

All the pressure is on the shooter. This is a read-and-react situation for the netminder. An early clue is where the shooter is carrying the puck. Is the puck to the side or in front? Side means shot. Front means deke.

First, think shot. Be well out beyond the crease and in line with the puck. Take away the shot. You want the shooter to deke. If there is an angle, the closer the shooter gets the more you play the forehand shot. Watch for the defense coming back: they can take one side away from the puck carrier.

Once the shooter comes into the 10-foot/3-m zone stick-handling with the puck in front, it's a deke. Now you have the edge. Hold your ground. Don't go for the deke. Make the puck carrier commit to one side or the other.

> ### NHL TIP
> "On breakaways, I'm thinking who the shooter is. As he gets closer, I judge his speed and try to be as patient as I can."
> CURTIS JOSEPH

Be well out of the net to take away the shot, but not too far to get back in . . .

The puck carrier is coasting in shooting position. Hold your ground . . .

The shooter decides to deke. Wait for him or her to commit, then react.

# Breakaways

Once the puck carrier has committed to one side, don't overreact. Often your opponent will tuck the puck under you as soon as you open your legs. Keep your stickblade on the ice and between your legs. Depending on your style, play the move with your pad or skateblade. Keep your glove ready for the flip shot.

The key in moving to one side or the other on a deke is to get the pad on that side down fast. And if you can get your pad down and then kick out, that's even better. Making the breakaway save can turn a game around. Nothing feels better.

### Point shots

How you play a point shot depends on what is going on around you. An unchecked opponent to your side forces you back into your net, to guard the back door. An unchecked opponent in front of you forces you to get as close as possible behind that player, to smother the deflection.

Remember, once your opponents are established in your zone—as in a power play—read the play. Try to stay on your feet. Let the puck play you.

### Faceoffs in your zone

Be ready for anything. How is your centre doing on draws? If the opposing centre has a forehand shot toward you, beware of a shot right off the drop.

## *In your zone*

Be well out for a point shot. Take away as much net as possible . . .

. . . until another opponent appears. You still play the shot, but cheat back into your net. Don't let that open player get behind you for the easy tip-in.

Most often, the opposing centre will try to draw the puck back to a shooter near the slot. How the centre holds a stick tells you a lot.
- Reversed lower hand = draw back.
- Normal grip + forehand toward you = shot.

Check your equipment during the pause. Make sure your foot straps aren't loose. Let the official know if you're not ready. Look at the centre before the puck drops to see which way he or she shoots. Make sure your centre checks with you before committing to the faceoff. Then focus—totally—on the drop of the puck.

## Wraparounds

When your opponents have possession behind your net, keep your stance. Do not turn around. Look back over your shoulders.

To get to the opposite post, T-push across in one push off the near post, then turn the toe of your lead skate inward so the puck can't be banked in off your skateblade. Move your stick ahead of you and past the far post, but keep the blade open (not parallel to the goal line) on the way across. This will prevent the puck carrier from banking the puck off your stick into the net. Turn your stickblade slightly out from the goalmouth on the way across and then turn it square to the puck carrier once it is outside the post.

Reach ahead with your stick as you move across. You can prevent passouts just by having your stick outside the post before you get there.

*T I P*
Never leave the post until you lose sight of the puck going the other way.

Kendall is waiting, skateblade against the post, as Will comes around from behind. No chance . . .

. . . so he goes the other way. Kendall is already there, ready to poke-check the puck off his stick.

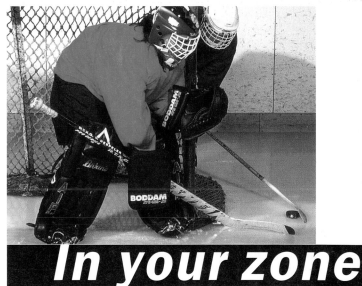

## In your zone

## In-your-zone checklist

- If you lose sight of the puck, get low. You can see through legs better than through bodies.
- When your team is losing faceoffs in your end, cheat toward the shooter—unless the opposing centre has a forehand shot on you.
- Are your teammates running around after the puck? Be cool. They need you more than ever now.
- Thank your defense for big plays. Nobody else will notice.

### Avoiding blocker rebounds

A skill that has almost disappeared from hockey is the art of taking the puck in your catcher after you've stopped it with your blocker.

### How to do it

Bring your mitt across, palm up, so the puck can drop into it after it hits your blocker. (You will have eliminated a rebound and can get a faceoff.) The trick is to field the puck with your blocker held vertically. That means getting your elbow up and out front, which is a good idea anyway. Once the puck is in your catching glove, you can keep the puck in play by dropping it where you want it.

If you want to avoid a transfer from glove to glove, let the puck hit your blocker and then smother it against your blocker with your open catching mitt. Maintain your balance.

# Rebounds

Prevent rebounds. Trap the puck on your blocker or let it drop into your catcher. Hold it for a faceoff.

Once you have the puck, get a faceoff by moving toward an opponent near the crease.

### Getting a faceoff

Once you've made the save and have the puck in your mitt, you might want to give your team a break. But there is no opponent near you, and the referee is waiting for you to play the puck.

With the puck safe in your catcher, move toward the nearest opposing player. Often, an opponent will skate toward you. That gives you a reason to hold the puck. Most times the referee will call a faceoff instead of the delay-of-game penalty you might have received.

## Be a leader

You are the only player on your team who sees the big picture. Help your teammates when trouble comes knocking, or when there's an opening they don't see. If you help keep your team organized in its own zone, that builds confidence, and it shows that you're in the game. Remember, though, you are yelling through a mask. Keep your message simple and positive. Be urgent, but under control. Never sound panicky.

- When your teammate has the puck and a checker is coming from the blind side or from behind, yell "*On* you!"
- When your teammate is double teamed, yell "*Two* to beat!"
- When a teammate is blocking your view, yell "Screen! Screen!"
- Call it out when your defense is outnumbered at the blueline. Yell "*Two*-on-one! *Three*-on-one!"

## Stay in the game

Don't just give your teammates the bad news.

- When a teammate has the puck in the open but no idea who might be around, yell "You got *time*!"
- To a teammate coming back for a loose puck, with his or her back to the play and no checker in sight, yell "*No* pressure!"
- Often your opponents will dump the puck to get a change. Let your teammate know. Yell "They're *chang*ing!"
- Watch the farthest official, who will call icings. Let your teammate know. Yell "Icing!" or, more important, "*No* call!"
- Let your team know when its power play is about to expire: bang your stick on the ice when there are five seconds left. Call out the name of your teammate nearest the penalty box.

> **N H L  T I P**
>
> "Many times the goaltender has to be a defenseman's eyes. One way is by telling the defense what to do, so they can make the right play to get the puck out of the zone."
>
> R O N   T U G N U T T

# Communication

## Be a good sport

It also pays to communicate with the officials. When they compliment you on a good save, say "Thanks." Let them know you appreciate good calls. Often, they will tell you how they work—and if a referee tells you he or she lets the players play, that's important information.

After the game, communicate with your opponents. Show them respect. Congratulate them. You know better than anyone on your team how good your opponents are. If it was a tight game, they deserve compliments as much as your team does. Shaking hands after the game is a chance to be a good sport.

It will happen. Sooner or later, you will faithfully follow your pre-game routine, visualize yourself playing the lights out, work up a healthy sweat in the warmup—and still be stone cold at the drop of the puck. But there are ways of finding out if you're not ready—before the scoreboard tells everyone else.

## What to do

- When you feel your upper-body sweat go cold, you've been standing around too long. Give yourself a pep talk. Don't think it, say it. Right out loud. Tell yourself you are asleep. Tell yourself to wake up. Find a two- or three-word piece of advice to repeat to yourself: "Give them nothing!" Or, "Get into it!" What you say is not that important. Saying it over and over is.
- Focus on the puck, wherever it is.
- Keep busy between shots. Check your equipment. Move around the net. Don't worry about looking silly. You'll look sillier fishing the puck out of your net.
- Try to play the puck—and make the right decision—on routine plays. Do the little things right.

# The mind game

### TIP
Don't dwell on the past. Move on. Be in the present. Your most important save is always the next one.

## Game time checklist

- Are you communicating with your defense? If you are in your shell, you are not in the game.
- Have you been lucky so far? The shooters won't be hitting the posts all night.
- Are you aware of the time on the clock?
- Are you just standing around while the puck is in the other end, or are you keeping busy?

## The puck is in the net

How you react to being scored on can make or break you as a goaltender. Remember, even the best goaltenders give up an average of one goal for every 10 shots. The trick is to make the next save. It helps to note how the goal was scored. Think for a moment how you might have played it differently, and then park those thoughts. Seal them off.

The single most important mental habit a goaltender can develop is to admit failure, learn from it and move on. The past is history, the future is a mystery and the present is a gift.

"For me, there is a huge difference between speed and quickness. Quickness is more of a reaction, a quick movement to the puck or a player in the corner."

JERE LEHTINEN

**NOBODY WILL TELL YOU** this, but almost all goalies buy their equipment for the way it looks, rather than for how it works. The great Russian goalie Vladislav Tretiak, for example, took up hockey because he liked the uniforms.

A goalie's equipment is part of his or her style and personality. Leg pads are made differently for stand-up or butterfly goalies. But all goalie equipment has to fit right in order to protect.

Goaltending equipment is expensive. It deserves care. One characteristic of good goalies is the way they care for their equipment. For goalies, more than most athletes, equipment you care for is equipment that takes care of you.

# *equipment*

## GOALTENDING

## Skates

Goalie skates come in two types: plastic shell with booties, and leather uppers with plastic reinforcements.

For hard-to-fit feet, the shell type offers the most flexibility. Some goalies also feel they offer better protection—and they last. Replace the booties, you've got new skates. Skates with leather uppers require a longer break-in period. But in the long run, for a standard foot, the break-in period will pay off in a better fit.

## Leg pads

Leg pads come in all sizes and shapes, with different styles for stand-up or butterfly goalies. Stand-up goalies use shorter pads. Pads for butterfly goalies wrap more padding inside the knees.

Kendall's pads have extra protection inside the knees.

Store your pads with the wettest part up, so they'll dry faster. The pros do.

These older pads are worn away inside the toes. Avoid this.

# *Skates & pads*

Look your pads over after every use. Use a good moisture repellant, especially around the foot area and down the inside of the pad, where a butterfly goalie's pads meet the ice. Moisture adds weight to pads. Store your pads upside down so they hold their shape and the wettest parts dry fastest; the pros do.

If your pads have toe straps, check them. Keep spares in your bag. Wrap tape around the middle of the toe strap to cushion impacts. Do the same at the point where the first (or first two) bottom-foot strap rubs on the skateblade supports.

### Trapper (catching mitt)

Your catching mitt is your most personal piece of equipment. It makes saves all by itself and seldom gives up rebounds. Why not give it some extra care? After games, stack four pucks in the pocket and wrap an elastic-velcro shinguard strap around it to deepen the pocket. Don't just toss it in your bag.

### Blocker

About all you have to worry about with a blocker is wearing holes in the inner fingers. Small holes actually help you grip the stick, but once they get larger, a bare finger on your stick is an invitation for a permanent disability. Get the holes fixed.

# Mitts & masks

Look for stiffness along the thumb and wrist guard of a used catching mitt.

Used blockers are fine if the glove palm is fully intact.

Michelle's goal mask and throat protector overlap, leaving no openings.

### Helmet/mask

This is one item where you can save money. Not every goalie needs a custom-painted pro-style mask. A helmet/cage combination can get the job done for about half the cost of a pro-style Fiberglas cage combination. Make sure all the screws and fasteners are tight before every game.

If you use a helmet/cage model, look for a cage with square, rather than rounded, bars and openings. Goalie coach Andy Moog says that a little extra padding in the sides and back doesn't hurt in making a slightly oversize—but CSA-approved—unit fit better.

It costs a lot of money to buy goaltending equipment, and a sure sign of a good goalie is how he or she takes care of it. Your gear spends a lot of time in your bag, so bag it right.

Packing your bag needs to become a routine, with everything going into its place. That way, if something is missing, you'll know right away. (If your skates go inside your bag, use skate guards to protect your other gear.)

Keep some spares on hand: toe straps, helmet fasteners, tape and an extra pair of socks. An oily rag in a zip-lock bag is ideal for cleaning off skateblades. On top of everything else, buy yourself a carpet sample. For a couple of bucks, you get your own mobile, carpeted dressing room stall.

**Figure out a good way to pack your equipment, and stick with it . . .**

**. . . so you'll notice if something is missing. A goalie really hates that.**

**Build strong off-ice routines. The games are crazy enough.**

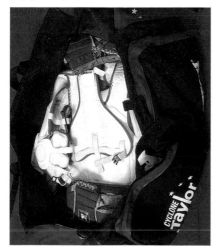

# Packing your bag

Of course, everything must come out between games. Set your equipment out to dry as soon as you return home. Make yourself do it every time. This is a good habit to develop, and it is one of the few times when you can think about how well you played.

If you won, try to think of something you learned. If you lost, try to find something you did right. Finally, what was the best moment of all? Remember that big save as you set your equipment out to dry, checking it for wear or damage. Give yourself credit. Be your own coach.

"All that is going through my mind in a power-play faceoff is to try and move the puck back. The longer you have the puck on the power play, the better."

MIKE MODANO

# SPECIAL
## TEAMS

**IT IS NOT UNUSUAL** to have 10 penalties or more called during a hockey game. These can add up to nearly half an hour with one team or the other having a huge advantage. No wonder the power-play and penalty-killing units are called Special Teams.

It takes special players to play on Special Teams: players who can protect the puck or check, players who skate hard both ways, players who like to prevent goals as much as score them.

In special team situations, you have to read and react when the puck changes hands. When the penalty killers get the puck, they go on offence. When that happens, the power play switches in a heartbeat to defense.

Here's what you need to know to be on the ice at those key moments.

### The basics

You know that there are differences between power plays and penalty killing. One difference is the number of players you have on the ice. But it's more important to know how power plays and penalty killing are the same. The key point to remember is that penalty-killing and power-play units both work with time and space; they just use them in different ways.

### On the power play

The power-play unit has a certain amount of time to work with, plus a little more space than when the sides are even. On a power play you need to use that time and space to try and score. The idea is to get the puck into the middle of your opponents' zone— the shooting zone—and take your shot.

## Give support

After passing, the forward on the boards creates pressure by moving into the slot for a return pass . . .

. . . while, inside the penalty-kill box, the original puck carrier takes the return pass.

### Penalty killing

Penalty killers work with time, too. They are trying to *stall* and *contain:* to hold things up. First, you forecheck, to keep the power-play unit in its defensive zone and contain it there, if possible. Once the power-play unit is set up in your zone, your penalty-killing unit will try to push the power play to the outside. On a penalty kill, your job is to keep the power-play unit out of the shooting zone. Then, once you get the puck, you can make the power-play unit chase *you.*

For a brief moment, while the referee delays calling the penalty, the attacking team can replace its goalie with an extra attacker. To get the extra attacker on the ice, two players must see the referee's arm signal. Your goaltender must see it and skate to the bench. (The team that is about to be penalized can not score; as soon as they get the puck, the whistle will sound.) The other player who must notice the referee's signal is the one who will replace the goalie on the ice. That player is usually the centre of the line going on the ice for the next shift.

### Delayed penalties checklist

- First, your goaltender must get to the bench. If you see a penalty about to be called but your goalie hasn't noticed, call your

Here, the bench is ready. Shout "Next centre!" as you get close.

The sixth attacker is off and running. Get your power play off to a great start.

A sharp goalie gives his team a lift by getting to the bench fast.

# *Delayed penalties*

goalie to the bench. When the goalie is within 10 feet/3 m of the bench, the extra attacker can go over the boards.

- One way to keep possession is to pass the puck to your point, who may decide to bring the puck back into the neutral zone. If that happens, it is important for those teammates on the ice to get back and give support to the puck carrier.
- Don't just stand around and celebrate when the referee is about to call a penalty against your opponents. There are things you can do to help your team score—*before* the ref blows the whistle.

**THE TRICK** to a successful power play is to make the best use of the extra players on the ice. The idea is to get a shot from the ideal scoring position—right in front of your opponents' net. With the advantage of one or more players, your power-play unit should be able to do that.

A top NHL power-play unit scores on just one in four chances; the best NHL penalty-killing units keep their opponents from scoring nine out of 10 times. So it is more likely the penalty will be killed than the power play will score. This means that for your team to score, your power play needs a plan of attack. A good power play is not just more players, it is more players with a plan.

# *power plays*

## S P E C I A L   T E A M S

## Getting the puck into the offensive zone

Most penalties are called on defenders, so power plays usually begin in the offensive zone. But, because penalty killers are allowed to ice the puck, many power-play scoring chances begin with players breaking out of their own zone. This means that the first thing to do on a power play is to get the puck into the offensive zone and control it there if necessary.

## How to do it

There are three ways you can bring the puck into the offensive zone: carry the puck in; chip the puck off the boards; or dump-and-chase. All three plays are easy—and effective. Remember: which play you choose depends on what you see at the blueline.

Carry the puck until you are checked. Don't pass until you have to. Get the puck deep . . .

. . . then make the pass to an open teammate. Remember: if you are being checked, somebody's open.

# The offensive zone

## Carry the puck in

The best way to get the puck into the offensive zone is to carry it in—skate the puck through the neutral zone until you are pressured. Your aim in getting the puck deep is to buy your teammates time to set up the power play. Once inside the offensive zone, there are a few good ways to get the puck to a teammate.

**Pass to an open teammate:** If you are crossing the blueline close to the boards, skate hard with the puck and make a sharp turn toward the boards. That should shake off any checker. Next, look to pass to a teammate deeper in the zone. If there is no one open, look to the near-side point.

**Pass behind the net:** If you have moved deep into the offensive zone and find yourself being double-teamed, pass behind the net off the end-boards to a teammate on the other side. If you are under pressure, chances are a teammate is free on the other side of the ice.

### Chip the puck off the boards

Your second option is to chip the puck off the boards past the defensive pressure. A teammate skating close to you can skate onto the loose puck and gain control deep in the zone.

# The offensive zone

The open teammate is often on the other side of the zone. Off the boards behind the penalty-killing team's net is a good idea.

Remember:
- Carry the puck until checked. If there is no pressure, go all the way to the net.
- Move up the ice as a unit. Support the puck carrier by being available for a pass.
- Never go offside on a power play. There's plenty of time.
- Once in the zone, you *want* defenders to attack you. This opens up passing lanes.
- Be aggressive. Be in control.

## Dump-and-chase

Sometimes penalty killers line up along their blueline, making it hard to carry the puck into their zone. When this happens, the best way to get the puck into their zone is to dump-and-chase. Make sure you are past the red centre-ice line. Flip the puck high and deep, then skate hard after it. The penalty killers have to turn around and get going, and may be slow getting to the puck; you and your teammates should beat them to the puck.

## Offensive zone checklist

- Read and react to what you see as you move through the neutral zone.
- Choose the right play (you have three choices) to get the puck into the offensive zone.

When your opponents are guarding their blueline, dump the puck. Shoot after you cross the centre-ice line . . .

. . . The winger on the other side must beat the defenseman to the puck and control it.

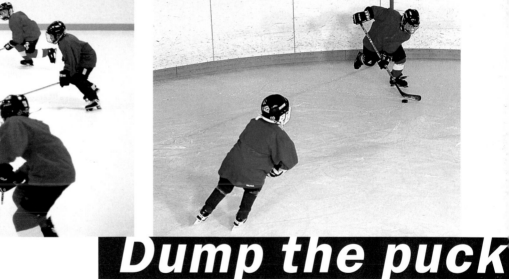

# *Dump the puck*

- Pressure the defensive team by skating hard into the zone, attracting checkers.
- Remember that if the team with the extra attacker can't get set up in the offensive zone, there is no power play. (A power-play unit will sometimes score on the rush. But a power-play unit is usually set up to match a penalty-killing unit player for player, and to outnumber them in a certain area: near the net, in the slot or in the shooting zone.)

The key power-play skill you need is the ability to see the ice and put the puck on the stick of the player most likely to score. That is a rare skill, even in the NHL. It is so rare that players who can fill that role are called power-play quarterbacks. One reason they are called that is because a successful power play usually requires set plays—planned out before the game, as in football. In football, most plays start with the quarterback handling the ball. In hockey, a good power play works the same way.

There are four key steps to most power plays:

**1.** Control and protect the puck.
**2.** Move the puck.
**3.** Get into the box.
**4.** Work the plan.

Master all four steps and you'll be a power-play quarterback.

# Quarterback the PP

This is Kellin Carson quarterbacking the power play, but it could be Paul Kariya . . .

. . . and with the puck controlled by the power-play unit, the next step is to get it to the point. Here, Kellin looks to the far post and his open teammate.

## Control and protect the puck

If the puck is *carried* over the blueline, your teammates must:
- Stay open and close by for quick, short passes.

If the puck is *dumped* in, your teammates must:
- Skate hard to the puck.
- Outnumber the defenders at the puck.
- Move the puck to the point. Or, if they can't move the puck,
- Protect the puck and wait for help.

## Use your teammates

On the power play, the puck carrier must pressure the defenders by moving the puck. To do that, the puck carrier must see open teammates. Each offensive player must:

- Provide a passing option for the puck carrier. Every pass means your team might lose the puck, so passes should be short, crisp and stick-to-stick.
- Work to offer a pass-receiving option. Beat your check.
- Adjust and offer close support when a teammate receives the puck. (On receiving the puck, the new puck carrier must protect it. Move to give support by being ready to receive the next pass.)

> **T I P**
> If you keep the puck moving it changes the point of attack—forcing players on a penalty kill to chase the puck.

Move the puck quickly, and know what you are going to do with it before it comes to you.

Teammates must move between penalty killers to create options for the puck carrier. Here, Dane Stevens makes the right choice—to pass.

# *Move the puck*

## Power-play checklist

- The breakout from your own zone must be smooth and according to plan, with players moving up the ice together.
- Movement through the neutral zone must be as a five-player unit to keep each penalty killer busy.
- Keep or gain control of the puck in the offensive zone.
- After the power play is set up in the offensive zone, play as a unit.
- Each player must move into the open spaces to create passing lanes for the puck carrier.

### Walkout lanes

A penalty-killing unit on a five-on-four must protect the shooting zone by forming a box. Your power-play unit must attack the box by moving the puck inside the box where the chances of scoring are high. A good way to do this is by moving into the box through the openings between defenders. On a five-on-four power play, there are five gaps between defenders, one for each power-play attacker. These are called "walkout lanes."

Two teammates, one with the puck, form a two-on-one against one defender. Either attacker can pressure the box by forcing the defender to make a choice. In committing to either attacker, the defender opens up a walkout lane, making it bigger. As the puck carrier, you read and react to the defender's choice, passing or keeping the puck. Either way, the puck moves into the box.

# Get into the box

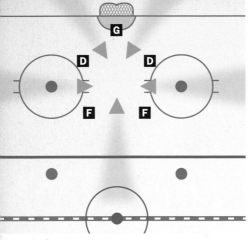

The openings between penalty killers in their box are called the "walkout lanes."

The point man moves the puck into the middle of the ice, trying to get to the shooting lane before the defender.

### Creating pressure

As a puck carrier and offensive player, you can enter these lanes to create pressure in front of the net—in two ways:
- You can carry the puck into the box. Or,
- You can pass the puck to a teammate and move into the lane for a return pass. This creates a two-on-one against the nearest defender. Play this situation as you would any two-on-one, by reading and reacting to the choices the defender must make.

Most power-play set-ups occur at the half-boards, near the outside of the faceoff circles. Usually, this is where the power-play quarterback will be. That's because there are so many passing options from this spot. From here, as the power-play quarterback you have several options to choose from:

- If your teammate in the middle is available, that's your first choice.
- Passing to the point is a safe choice that moves the puck toward the middle.
- Passing to the low forward puts pressure on the strong-side defenseman. (The strong side is the side where the puck is.) It also opens up your chance of another pass, into the slot.
- Or you could move toward the blueline, move down low or try to carry the puck into the slot and see if a defender will bite.

> **T I P**
> One way to keep the puck away from your opponents' goalie is to dump it into a corner.

Always be ready to shoot on the point. Here, the defender over-plays the passer, so Kellin is open to shoot . . .

. . . To give himself a better shooting angle, he drags the puck into the middle. He can now shoot toward the net.

# Work the plan

## Read and react

Which play you should make depends on what the two defenders on your side of the box are doing. If one of the defenders moves toward you, the quarterback, you could direct the puck to the area the defender just left, to take advantage of that open space.

By passing the puck and moving into the slot for a return pass, you force the defender to make a choice. As in a two-on-one, you or your teammate will be open to take the pass and shoot.

### Setting it up

Most goals scored on the power play start from point shots. Here are two simple plays to set up the point shooter.

### Move to the middle and shoot

The power-play quarterback passes to the near, or strong-side, point. The point shooter moves to the middle of the ice and shoots. Both the low forward and the quarterback enter the box to look for a rebound. If the defender at the top of the box moves along the blueline with the point shooter, the quarterback is open and should get a return pass from the point.

# The point shot

A point shooter must make quick choices. Pass or shoot? This defender is off his line to the net...

...so he shoots. Shooting low makes the goalie handle the shot with his or her stick. Rebounds are more likely.

### The one-timer

Instead of shooting, the strong-side defenseman takes the pass and moves the puck to his or her partner for a one-timer shot. The pass should arrive just ahead of the receiver, and on the ice.

As a point shooter you always have the option of shooting to the side of the low forward for the easy tip-in. All your point shots should be low to create rebounds. As Wade Redden says, "The one thing you don't want to do is miss the far post—the puck will hit the boards and go around the zone."

Remember: If your shot line to the net is blocked, get the puck deep along the boards. A blocked point shot can result in a breakaway on your net.

**"It took me years to realize that hockey is played with the lower body. My off-seasons are geared toward leg strength. I increase my quickness through plyometrics."**

KEITH PRIMEAU

Many power plays begin with faceoffs in the offensive zone These might be the most important faceoffs of the entire game. All the basics of faceoffs apply in this case, and some are critical.

Learn from faceoffs against the same opponent early in the game. For example, how does the other centre grip the stick? Remember: As a centre you must make sure that each of your teammates is positioned in the correct spot before going to the dot. Take your time. Watch the official's hand. Have a plan.

Here are three ways to win a faceoff:

### Get the puck to the shooter

In offensive-zone draws, the centre will usually try to get the puck back to the point or to a shooter in the slot. The easier play to

# PP faceoffs

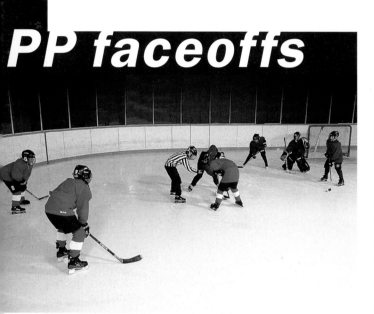

Every power-play faceoff is important. This centre has three options: the point, the slot or the left-winger...

... The penalty-kill centre is quicker, so the power-play centre attacks his stick.

make is to the point, but a hard scoop directly backward can miss the target (the point's stickblade), forcing the power-play unit to gain entry to the zone again. A better plan is to block your opponent's stick, get control and move the puck to the shooter.

The moment you release the puck, go to the front of the net.

### One-time the puck

If the faceoff is on the side that gives you a forehand shot on goal, think about doing just that. One-time the puck when it hits the ice. This works best if your opponent is holding his or her stick with the blade pointed toward the half-boards—the same side as yours. Often the goalie will cheat toward the middle and the shooter, leaving the short side open. Take a look. Go to the net for your own rebounds.

## Move the puck ahead

Sometimes the best plan on a power-play faceoff in the offensive zone is to move the puck ahead, rather than drawing it back. This is a great idea if you have been losing most of your faceoffs. Let your teammates know what you have in mind. The trick is to get past your opponent and regain possession, usually in the corner. If you lose the draw and a penalty-kill defenseman has the puck, forecheck hard.

> ### N H L  T I P
> "The best power-play faceoff situation, for me, is in their zone, on the left-hand side of the rink. What I try to do is lay it back to one of our defensemen, to set up the power play."
> **M I K E  M O D A N O**

Be a solid tripod—by using your feet and stick. Watch the official's hand. The penalty-kill centre is swinging left to protect the puck...

...so the power-play centre attacks his stick. You can't win every faceoff, but you can avoid losing most of them.

**PP faceoffs**

## PP faceoff tips

- Get your teammates set up the way you want them.
- Take a deep breath, and place your stickblade on the dot. Watch the referee's hand.
- If the faceoff is on your forehand side in the offensive zone, one-time it on the net. Go for the short side.
- Keep shots off the faceoff low. Think rebound.
- Don't always draw the puck back. Go forward sometimes. Keep them guessing.
- Never bug the ref. The referee gets the last word.

Some goalies see the power play as vacation time. But there's a lot to do when your team has the advantage. You can be the one who triggers the power play, and the one who makes sure it ends safely. By staying in the game when your team has the manpower edge, you can help prevent a shorthanded goal. If you can pass the puck you might even get an assist. Here's what to work on.

## Staying in the game

Keep faith with your teammates by zeroing in on the puck— all the way to the other end of the rink. Most penalties called on your opponents will be in their zone. So be alert for easy-to-spot calls, like tripping, slashing or high-sticking. But remember: Do not call penalties for the referees. You know how refs hate that.

# PP goaltending

Make the effort to stay in the game when your team is playing in the other end . . .

. . . If your teammate is the victim and the ref's arm is up, you're outta there . . .

. . . If your team has the puck and there's no whistle, make tracks for the bench.

> ### TIP
> As a goalie, be the power-play trigger: watch for penalties being called and skate to the bench.

When you think you see a penalty, watch for the referee to raise his or her arm. When that happens, if your team is controlling the puck, hustle to the bench. Be ready to stop during the first few strides, just in case you are wrong, your opponents get control and no whistle is blown. Once you commit, skate hard.

Your teammates will usually be facing away from you, watching the play. So if nobody on the bench sees you coming, shout "Next centre!" You want the centre of the next line to replace you on the ice.

## Watch for turnovers

On the power play, there is always plenty of warning when something goes wrong. It usually happens two zones away from you. Danger signs are cross-ice passes anywhere in the zone—but especially at the blueline—or a point man pinching or shooting into a checker's shinpads. Often you can see the turnover before it happens.

Turnovers on penalties often catch the power-play unit going the wrong way, so they often lead to breakaways or two-on-ones. But you do have time to get ready. Take a moment to be sure of your positioning. Commit to the shooter. Think of yourself as the equalizer.

> **T I P**
> Pay attention to the little things: control rebounds, stay tight to the post, keep the play moving, watch the clock.

Power plays often give up great scoring chances. On two-on-one rushes, be high but not outside your crease. Take the shooter.

Point shots get blocked and turn into breakaways. Be ready. Make the shooter make the first move.

# PP goaltending

## Take control

When play is in the offensive zone, set yourself up a little further out of the net than usual. Think of yourself as being in control of the space within the faceoff dots and the back-boards. You are in charge here. Talk to your teammates.

If you can handle the puck, you can save your teammates valuable seconds on the power play by stopping shootarounds and moving iced pucks up to your defensemen. Look around. Know what you intend to do with the puck before it gets to you. Then watch the puck into your glove or onto your stick.

The rules for goaltenders making passes are the same as for anyone else. Always make eye contact with the receiver before you pass. Look to see what side of the body the receiver's stick is on, and make a smooth, firm pass to that side. Sweep the puck, don't jerk it. Try to make the short, easy pass directly up the ice.

### Making the big play

When you field a dump-in or an iced puck, chances are the penalty killers are changing. When you have the puck on your stick and feel no pressure, look for a teammate on the near side of the centre-ice line, on the opposite side of the ice from the benches. If that teammate is alone, make that pass.

# The sixth attacker

Make eye contact with the receiver before you pass the puck. Hit the tape.

The home-run pass: The penalty-kill unit is changing. Look for your teammate . . .

Let your teammates know the bad guy is back.

**TIP**

When passing, aim for the tape on your receiver's stick. Follow through by pointing the end of your stickblade where you want the pass to go.

### When it's over, it's over

Nothing gives a penalty-killing unit more of a lift than a scoring chance just as the penalty expires. You can help prevent that. Let your teammates know when there are 10 seconds left in the power play. Bang the blade of your stick on the ice.

When your teammates are in the offensive zone, the penalized player often leaves the box and returns to the ice behind their backs. Watch for the returning player to leave the box and warn the point man on that side, *by name,* if the other team is taking control of the puck.

SPECIAL TEAMS
# *penalty killing*

**ALTHOUGH A GOOD POWER-PLAY** unit scores on one out of four penalties, a good penalty-killing unit can kill off nine out of 10 penalties. That means effective penalty killers are vital to any team. So if you want to be on the ice with the game on the line, be in on the penalty kill.

Often the most skilled offensive players are chosen for the power play, while the ones who always do the job go out when the team is down a player or two. There is more at stake on the penalty kill. And there is more enjoyment, not only because of a penalty-killing unit's higher success rate but because your teammates know you made a difference.

A good penalty-killing unit allows your team to play harder—all the time.

Coaches look for hockey smarts—the ability to read the play—in penalty killers. On a penalty kill, you need to know when to wait and when to attack the puck. You need to spot a turnover sooner than others do, and switch to offense while your opponents are still going the wrong way.

Next comes speed. It takes players who can skate well to make up for a missing player. Speed creates pressure on the power play. Speed cancels out mistakes. It turns the tables. Even when you don't have the puck yourself, your speed makes your opponents nervous. You can forecheck harder knowing you have the wheels to get back before the power-play unit gets to your zone.

# Read and speed

Speed and positioning on the penalty kill are key. Here, Luke Holowaty sees Brooks Stillie, who is coming hard . . .

. . . they meet at the puck. Luke can't control it. Brooksie wins—this time.

## What you need to know

There are two basic ways to kill penalties: passive and aggressive. Your coach will decide how your team should kill penalties, depending on your unit's ability to read and react, its speed and its puck skills. Passive means good positioning, taking few risks and waiting for the power play to make a mistake. Aggressive means attacking the power-play unit at every turn: forechecking its breakout, getting in the way through the neutral zone and standing up at your blueline.

Only after read and speed do we get to puck skills. For a smart player who can skate, the penalty-killing unit is the place to shine.

## Defending in the offensive zone

Like all defensive aspects of hockey, a good penalty kill begins in the offensive zone, with forechecking. In any system, if you are the first forechecker into the zone you need to do three things:

**1. Read** how well the puck carrier is controlling the puck. If he or she is not handling the puck well, go hard to the puck.

**2. Choose** an angle on the puck carrier that the forechecker behind you can read. Take away one lane. If you are coming along the boards, seal off the boards and force a pass up the middle. Your teammate will read and react by moving into the open lane.

**3.** If the puck carrier retreats behind the net, **go** to the front of the net high in the slot area, and wait.

The power-play defenseman looks up-ice, but the forechecker is in the way. The defenseman then skates behind his own net to wait for help . . .

... while the forechecker waits out front, letting the defenseman waste seconds of his own power play.

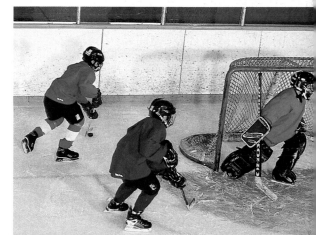

# Forechecking

## Once the power play breaks out

Get back fast. Pick up your check in the neutral zone. If the wings are covered and the defense stands up at the blueline, many cross-ice passes will end up on defenders' sticks. Often the puck carrier (seeing the defense waiting) will slow down at your blueline and the others will go offside.

With both defensemen standing up at the blueline, easy entry into your defensive zone is denied. Remember: Your defense can only stand up at the blueline if they see that both pass-receiver forwards are covered by backcheckers. Otherwise they must back off to prevent those forwards from sneaking behind the defense.

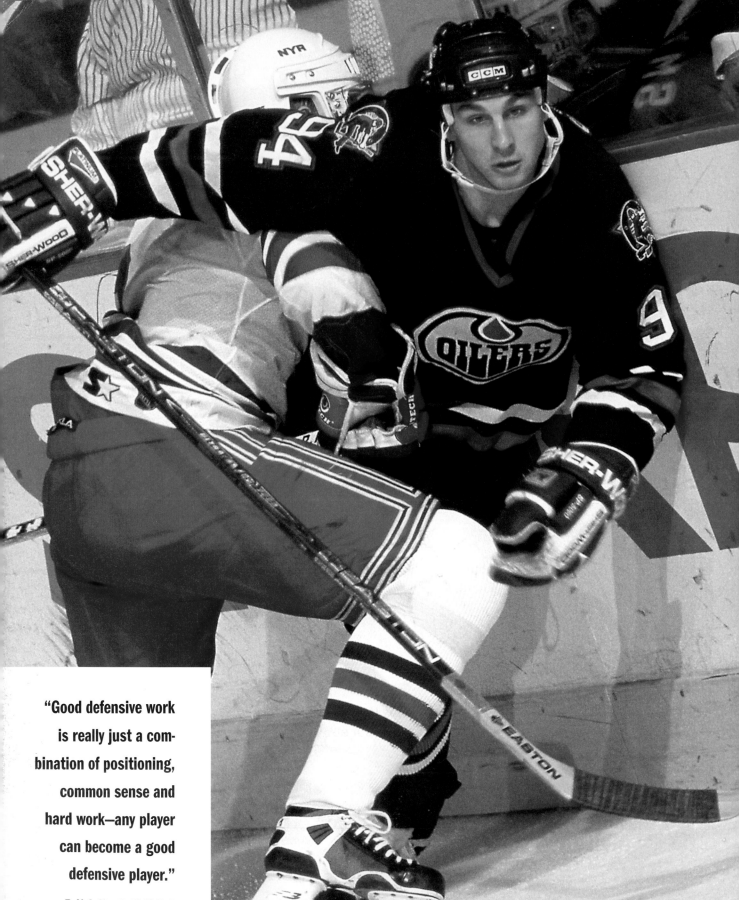

> "Good defensive work is really just a combination of positioning, common sense and hard work—any player can become a good defensive player."
>
> RYAN SMYTH

Once in a while, despite your best efforts, the power-play unit will set up in your zone with good puck possession. A good way to look at being on the penalty kill in your own zone is that you have your opponents where you want them. They are in your zone, where your goalie evens the numbers on a five-on-four penalty kill.

Think of yourself and your teammates as having an advantage. Your job is easy: Just keep the power play out of the shooting zone.

## The walkout lanes

Think of yourself as checking two opponents: the ones on either side of you. You need to position yourself to take away the walkout lanes between you and the teammate on each side of you. Together, you and your teammates form a box. All four of you

**N H L  T I P**

"Stay out of any confusion down low. Be aware of where the opposing player is in front of the net and clear him out, while making sure that your goaltender can see the puck."

C H R I S   C H E L I O S

Good positioning has Brooksie covering two power-play forwards . . .

Brooksie reads the play, blocks the pass and goes after the puck carrier.

A quick poke-check does the trick.

# In your zone

have your sticks on the ice, blocking the passing lanes your opponents want to move the puck through. Have your stick on the same side as the puck carrier's forehand.

We call it the "walkout lane" because the aim of the power-play unit is to get a player into your box—with the puck. A player inside your box with the puck is in the shooting zone. You and your penalty-killing unit are trying to cut off passes, clog the middle and prevent scoring chances.

Most of the time, the two forwards killing off a five-on-four penalty are checking the points, while the defensemen are in charge down low. But you are really covering two players. The reason for thinking you have two opponents (the ones on either side of you) to check is this: If one of them has the puck, his or her best play is a give-and-go, with the next player on either side breaking into the middle of your penalty-killing unit's box. That's a two-on-one, with you as the "one."

How do you defend a two-on-one? You stay between the two attacking players and block the pass. Anywhere near the net, defend against the pass and let your goalie take the shooter. As soon as an opponent gets inside the box, you and your teammates must back into the middle and down, toward your net. You remain in a box, but a smaller box.

# Think two-on-one

Two penalty killers and the goalie are covering one side of the zone—even-up.

Even if the power-play unit gets the puck to the shooter closest to the net (which they have done here), everyone on the power play is covered. The goalie has the shooter.

## When you get the puck

If you intercept the puck on the penalty kill, and you are not under pressure, hold onto it for a moment. Don't just hammer the puck up-ice. Are you being checked? If not, keep the puck. Look around. Is a teammate breaking out of the defensive zone? Is the power-play unit changing shifts? If you are confident of your puck-protection skills, carry the puck into your opponents' zone. Make the power-play unit come after you. Run the clock down. If you feel pressure you can still ice it.

## Blocking the shot

Blocking a point shot can hurt, but it can also get you a break-away. Line up with the puck, not the shooter's body. Stay square; never turn to the side. Expect the puck to bounce off your shin pads past the shooter. Skate hard past the shooter. Push the puck ahead of you, and carry it in the shooting position as soon as you reach the circles.

Never leave your feet, except when you are desperate. A shooter will often fake the shot to get you out of position. Hold your ground.

## In-your-zone checklist

- In the defensive zone, watch your check closely. Look for signs of weakness. Does he or she want the puck? Does your check receive the puck cleanly? If the answers are yes, back off and

*N H L   T I P*

"On the penalty kill you have to build on smaller things, like not giving them room to work. Keeping them away from scoring positions is important. Try not to allow one-timers."

J E R E   L E H T I N E N

Block the point shot with your shin pads and it will often bounce past the point man . . .

The goalie evens-up a two-on-one. The defenseman denies the pass, the goalie takes the shooter. It's really a two-on-two.

# In your zone

position yourself to block passing lanes. If the answers are no (your check fumbles the puck or wants to get rid of it), attack.
- Keep your stick active, placing it at the side of your body— blocking potential passing lanes.
- Let the power-play unit move the puck around the outside of your zone for the entire two minutes if they want. Deny them one place: the mid-ice lane from the blueline in. A point shot from the middle of the ice is a good scoring chance.

## You can do it

Being two players down is not a death sentence. Usually the three players chosen to kill off a five-on-three are the team's best. They know that killing off a five-on-three can turn a game around. As for the power-play unit, it has too much of a good thing. It is expected to score; if its players can be kept off the scoreboard for even half a minute, they will be upset.

Killing any penalty gives a team a lift, but killing off a five-on-three changes a game's momentum almost like an unexpected goal does. Being chosen to be one of those three skaters on the ice is an honour, and it helps to know that the closer to your net the power play gets, the closer to even the numbers are.

# Five-on-three

A five-on-three power play is not a death sentence. Stay in position and let the power-play unit give you the puck. A pass through the slot invites the penalty-killing unit to take the puck and go the other way.

## Forecheck hard

It is always a good idea on a five-on-three to give the power-play unit a chance to hand you the puck. The single forward swings into the offensive zone, turns with the puck carrier and leaves the zone to pick up a wing. With that wing covered, the defense is now at even strength with the power-play forwards. Each can take one forward at the defense's blueline. If the forechecker picks up the power-play unit's centre, the same matchups are there.

Remember: If the power-play unit dumps the puck, the defense has to hustle back. If the defense gets there first and clears the puck, the power play has to start out again.

When the other team has control of the puck in your zone, there are three ways to play the triangle in a five-on-three power play.

**Standard triangle:** The most common triangle puts the forward at the apex, in the slot, with the defensemen where they would be in a four-player box: just inside the faceoff circles, about even with the dots. The forward covers the high slot and the points. When there isn't much pressure on them, the points will often move in. When that happens, look for the defense-to-defense pass that can be deflected or intercepted.

**Rotating triangle:** The forward at the point of the triangle tries to take away the defense-to-defense pass with his stick in the lane. In case that pass gets across, the weak-side defender, positioned

Close to the net, the three penalty killers have the advantage. The closer to the net, the more important the goalie becomes.

The forward on this five-on-three is blocking the passing lane to the uncovered player.

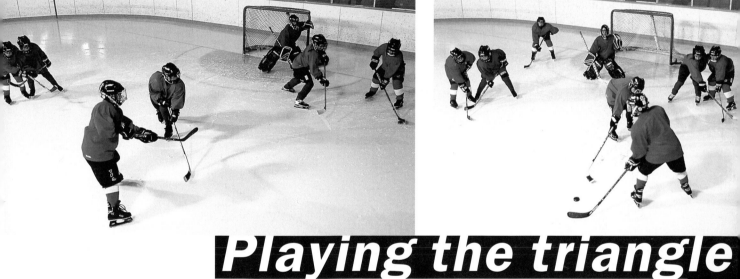

# *Playing the triangle*

close to the slot, must move out to defend against a point shot. The forward then drops back to take a position low on the triangle. This way the penalty-killing unit keeps pressure on the puck and lends support close to its own net.

**Sliding triangle:** Not every five-on-three has to be killed by two defensemen and one forward. A triangle with a single defenseman and two forwards works just as well to keep pressure on the points. The defenseman moves in front of his or her net from post-to-post, depending on what side the puck is on. The forwards move in and out: the forward on the strong-side out, the weak-side forward in, keeping an eye on the power-play forwards down low.

"You can work to develop your speed, but it's usually something you're born with. If you don't have speed, you have to work on your other skills."

BRIAN ROLSTON

## Stay confident

When you are outnumbered, every faceoff has a life-or-death feel to it. But winning faceoffs cleanly on the penalty kill is extra-important—especially in your own zone. There are two reasons. First, a lost faceoff in your own zone often leads to a close-in scoring chance for the power play. Second, penalty killers get tired quickly, and often the only way to get a change is to freeze the puck—which means another faceoff in your own zone.

## Study your opponent

Some coaches will allow you to watch your opposing centre on the first few faceoffs of the game, or on early draws at centre ice, to see how your opponent likes to take them. Also, watch faceoffs from the bench to see how the officials handle the puck.

> **N H L   T I P**
>
> "You're never going to win every faceoff, but if there is one place where you don't want to lose one, it's in your own zone. If you lose the faceoff, your job isn't over. Make sure the other centre man doesn't go to the net unopposed."
>
> S T E V E   R U C C H I N

Before you put your stick down, have a plan. Be prepared for anything. Watch the ref's hand.

The red power-play centre is winning the faceoff by reacting faster. The blue centre must block his opponent's way to the net.

# PK faceoffs

## Take charge

Faceoffs are one time when the centre is in charge on the ice. On a defensive-zone faceoff, make sure your teammates are where you want them to be. Never go to the dot without checking your teammates. Finally, check your goalie. Once you put your stick down, take a deep breath to relax and concentrate. Look at the puck in the official's hand out of the corner of your eye.

And remember: Whether you win or lose a faceoff, you can always prevent your opposing centre from going to the net.

### Read and react

All faceoffs are different, even on a penalty kill. How you need to handle a penalty-kill faceoff each time depends on how you have been doing against your opponent so far, where the faceoff was called and how you usually win them. In your own zone, it is often more important not to lose faceoffs than to win them cleanly. Go for your opponent's stick.

### PK faceoff tips

■ The best penalty-kill faceoff result is a clean draw back to the corner, away from the net. The defenseman can ice the puck or start a breakout by moving it to you, his or her partner or up the boards. Use the reverse lower-hand grip and draw straight back.

# PK faceoffs

The power-play centre attacks the penalty-kill centre's stick. The puck is up for grabs . . .

. . . so the penalty-kill centre skates into his opponent, pushing him off the puck. A teammate has control of the puck and can waste time or ice it.

> **TIP**
> If your opponent attacks your stick, use your leg on that side to protect it.

■ One way to not lose an important faceoff is to rotate your leg on your opponent's forehand side around the puck to protect it. Lean into your opponent, and use your skateblade to poke the puck back. Another way to neutralize your opponent is to lift his or her stick and kick the puck back.

■ When your opponent lines up on his or her forehand and has a direct shot on net, you are in a defensive position. Attack your opponent's shaft above the blade or jam the blade itself. Try to stay between your opposing centre and your team's net, in case the shot gets through and there's a rebound.

## Be prepared

As a goalie, nobody has to tell you what to do when your team is shorthanded. This is the time for you to step up and be the equalizer. A smart goalie can improve the penalty-killing unit's chances of holding the fort when it's surrounded and outnumbered.

You have to use all the tricks in your bag on a penalty kill. Save your energy. Stay on your feet. Be ready for rebounds. Don't give up on screen shots—in fact, expect them. Get your head down and look through the legs in front.

Most important, never blame anyone else when the other guys score. It takes at least two mistakes—one of them yours—to add up to a goal. The penalty-killing unit works hard in front of you, so be its biggest backer.

### T I P
Think of penalties as your chance to shine. Welcome the puck into your zone. Let it come to you.

Never use screens as an excuse. Keep your eyeballs on the puck. You can see better through legs than bodies.

Tory Malinoski helps his penalty killers by turning low shots into the corners—avoiding costly rebounds.

# PK goaltending

Penalties take a lot out of goaltenders; the intensity that penalties require is why working out pays off. Mike Richter ran around the Madison Square Garden ice-level hallway before every home game. Be like Mike.

## Don't overreact

Remember: Two or five minutes can be an eternity. So don't overreact. Take it one shot at a time. Don't come out as far on point shots as you would at other times—if the shot goes wide it can be tipped in by the low forward behind you.

## How to play it

Once the play gets close to your net, stay between the posts and play the shooter as always, but expect the pass. You can make the shooter pass by being in position and moving sideways. The more passes the better. Sooner or later the power-play unit will give your team the puck. If you are in position, often you won't have to make the save because the shooter won't take the shot.

Turn aside low shots. Be happy when the points shoot high. Once the puck is in your glove you can relax.

Take every break you can get. Have a drink of water during each stop in play. And, while you're doing that, tell yourself that the most important save is the next one. Every chance you get, any time you have doubts, freeze the puck. It doesn't just stop the play, it also takes at least a couple of seconds off the clock when the referee hesitates to blow the whistle.

# PK goaltending

Point shots that can be seen and aren't deflected don't often score. Tory's penalty-kill teammates are keeping the power play out of his way...

...but no penalty-killing unit is perfect. Sometimes goalies have to make big saves.

**T I P**

Call "Time!" if you are not ready for a faceoff. Do it before the linesman is set to drop the puck.

## Be alive on faceoffs

If part of your penalty-killing plan is to break up the penalty by getting faceoffs, make sure they don't backfire. If you are facing the centre's forehand shot, watch for it. Most times, the centre will try to get the puck to the shooter in the slot. Most shots from there are screened. Be prepared for the screen shot. Don't ever make it an excuse.

## Handle the puck

Stopping the puck behind the net on shootarounds is extra-important on the penalty kill. Learn to expect shootarounds if your penalty-killing unit is clogging up the blueline. Make the stop and then look to see who's coming. It's a plus for your team if you can flip the puck around the boards or out of the zone. But don't try it in a game until you know you can do it every time.

When you have the puck in your glove and an unchecked team-mate is on his or her way, set the puck down for an easy pickup.

## Stay in touch with your teammates

Some goalies go into a shell under pressure. But you are the only one on your team who can see most of the zone. Let the defense know when there's an unchecked opponent nearby. Often, the low

> **N H L  T I P**
>
> "As the goalie on the penalty kill, I try to communicate with the other players on the ice. I let them know whether they have time or if there's pressure. Being vocal is very important."
>
> R O N   T U G N U T T

Even the best power plays don't often get chances like this. Tory moves across with the shooter.

This two-on-one, like all two-on-ones, is actually a two-on-two. The second defender is the goalie. Tory plays the shooter.

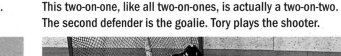

# PK goaltending

forward on the power play lurks beside the weak-side post. Tell your defenseman. As the penalty winds down to the last 30 seconds, let your penalty-killing unit know how much time is left. Often the defense will turn their backs on checkers to race for the puck. If there's a checker right behind, yell "Man on you!"

If there are two opposing checkers along the boards, shout "Two to beat!" When your teammate gets control of the puck and an opponent is coming from behind, yell "Behind you!" Try to keep your instructions to two or three words.

# The NHL Way Team

## OUR PLAYERS

Daniel Birch
Jesse Birch
Kellin Carson
Shae Dehaan
Tyler Dietrich
Nicolas Fung
Michael Garagan
Tyler Hansen
Brandon Hart
Will Harvey
Dylan Herold
Luke Holowaty
Brad Irving
Tara Khan
Derek MacKenzie
Jaysen Mah
Tory Malinoski
Michelle Marsz
Brian Melnyk
David Mercer
Lance Quan
Shayne Russell
Keith Seabrook
Jordan Sengara
Dane Stevens
Brooks Stillie
Rob Tokawa
Kendall Trout
Scott Tupper

## OUR COACHING ADVISORY STAFF

**Paul Carson**, director of development, Hockey Canada (Calgary)

**Pat Quinn**, head coach, the Toronto Maple Leafs; two-time winner of the Jack Adams Trophy as NHL Coach of the Year

**Marc Crawford**, head coach, the Vancouver Canucks

**Ken Hitchcock**, head coach, the Philadelphia Flyers

**Dave King**, former head coach, the Calgary Flames and the Columbus Blue Jackets

**Peter Twist**, author of *Complete Conditioning for Ice Hockey* (Human Kinetics, 1997)

**Terry Bangen**, special consultant to the Dallas Stars

**Ian Clark**, goaltending coach, the Vancouver Canucks

**Barb Aidelbaum**, power skating coach and skating director, the Arbutus Club, Vancouver, B.C.

**Jack Cummings**, hockey coordinator, the Hollyburn Country Club, West Vancouver, B.C.

**Bill Holowaty**, still the third-highest scorer in UBC Thunderbirds history; played in the Japanese pro league with the Siebu Lions

**Ken Melnyk**, author of the Hockey Skills Development Program for Tykes and Atoms in the Delta, B.C., minor hockey program

## PHOTOGRAPHY

Photography by Stefan Schulhof/Schulhof Photography, except:

Photos by Bruce Bennett Studios: pp. ii, 33, 36, 58, 104, 115, 148 by Bruce Bennett · pp. 4, 34, 71, 90, 99, 120, 133 by Jim McIsaac · pp. 8, 11 by Wen Roberts · p. 142 by John Giamundo

Photos by NHL Images: p. 49 by Kent Smith · p. 64 by Tim DeFrisco

Photo by Jessica Bushey/Vancouver Canucks: p. 12